DETROIT

BY LISA D'AMOUR

★

★

DRAMATISTS
PLAY SERVICE
INC.

DETROIT received its world premiere at the Steppenwolf Theatre Company in Chicago, Illinois, opening on September 9, 2010. It was directed by Austin Pendleton; the set design was by Kevin Depinet; the costume design was by Rachel Anne Healy; the lighting design was by Kevin Rigdon; and the original music and sound design were by Josh Schmidt. The cast was as follows:

BEN .... Ian Barford
MARY .... Laurie Metcalf
KENNY .... Kevin Anderson
SHARON .... Kate Arrington
FRANK .... Robert Breuler

DETROIT received its New York City premiere at Playwrights Horizons, opening on August 24, 2012. It was directed by Anne Kauffman; the set design was by Louisa Thompson; the costume design was by Kaye Voyce; the lighting design was by Mark Barton; the sound design was by Matt Tierney; and the production stage manager was Lisa Ann Chernoff. The cast was as follows

BEN .... David Schwimmer
MARY .... Amy Ryan
KENNY .... Darren Pettie
SHARON .... Sarah Sokolovic
FRANK .... John Cullum

CHARACTERS

BEN — Raised in the United States, somewhere inland: Kansas City, maybe Denver. He worked at one bank for five years and another bank for six years. Recently laid off from his job.

MARY — Raised in the United States, somewhere inland: Kansas City, maybe Denver. Met Ben after work at a happy hour, when he was working in a bank, and she was working as a paralegal assistant. Now she works as a paralegal at a small law firm.

KENNY — Raised in several cities in California until he was twelve or thirteen when his parents finally split up and he moved to Omaha with his mom. Now he works as a warehouse manager. Fresh out of major substance abuse rehab.

SHARON — Raised in Tucson, Arizona, until she was nine, when she and her mother moved to Columbus, Ohio, for two years and then to Indianapolis, where she went to high school. In her junior year her mother moved back to Arizona with her boyfriend, and Sharon lived with her best friend to finish school. Now Sharon works at a phone bank, answering customer service calls. Fresh out of major substance abuse rehab.

FRANK — Two generations older than the other characters. Maybe he's in his late seventies, early eighties? But he's spry, the kind of man who's been fixing his roof and rewiring the electricity on his house and taking care of his impeccable lawn for many years. He's happy.

PLACE

Not necessarily Detroit. However, we are in a "first ring" suburb outside of a mid-sized American city. These are the suburbs that comprise the first "ring" of houses outside the city proper. They were built perhaps in the late fifties, smaller houses, perhaps of outdated design. The kind of house many people today would consider a "starter house" or a house you would want to purchase, live in, and keep your eye on the lot next door so you could buy that, knock both houses down and build a double-lot house.

TIME

Now.

CASTING NOTE

When I wrote the play, I imagined Mary, Ben, Sharon and Kenny to be around thirty-four years old. I've since realized that there is some flexibility in terms of the ages of the characters. For example, the show can be cast with Mary and Ben a little older, in their forties, and Sharon and Kenny younger, in their late twenties, early thirties. It's also possible that Kenny is quite a bit older than Sharon. I just ask that directors consider how the age of the characters reverberates through the whole script: The focus of the story can shift quite a bit depending on how old they are.

SET NOTE

This play is set in the front and back yards of the characters' houses. There is a way to produce the play by setting it only in the back yards by cutting certain lines and adding a few lines. See the Addendum at the back of the book.

Plywood has a lifespan of 40 years. Over time, the glue that holds plywood together dries up. Then, walls buckle, split and peel. Panels pop loose. Rooms, doors and windows morph into trick-or-treat versions of themselves.

—Herbert Muschamp,
New York Times, *October 19, 1997*

Dogs, by this same logic, bark at what they cannot understand.

—Heraclitus

DETROIT

Lights up.

Sharon and Kenny are in Mary and Ben's back yard. They sit in newish looking lawn chairs — part of a set from maybe Home Depot. Mary struggles to get a patio umbrella to go up as she speaks — it's in the middle of the table and it's heavy. There is a grill nearby.

MARY. And the man with the birthmark looked up and slid a handwritten receipt across the table to me. He said, "Is there anything else I can help you with?" and I said no thank you and I turned and walked out onto the wooden pier and I saw a very old seagull swoop down into the water and eat a fish.

SHARON. How did you know it was old?

MARY. I just knew.

KENNY. And the bank was an old card table on the edge of an abandoned boardwalk?

MARY. And all the deposits went into an Adidas shoe box the banker kept under the table.

SHARON. They make those shoes in Germany. I went there for a week on this high school trip and everyone wanted to buy them. We all thought they were cheaper over there. I didn't buy any.

MARY. *(Under her breath.)* Shit. Shit shit shit.

KENNY. Can I help you with that?

MARY. No I'll be right back. *(Mary goes inside. Kenny and Sharon sit in the chairs in silence. They look hardly even look at each other. They take in the sounds of this new landscape: birds. A lawnmower in the distance. A clanging sound, like someone fixing something. A siren that we hear and quickly fades. Mary comes out with Ben following her. Ben has a pan full of meat, some kind of steaks. Mary is kind of in a tizzy.)* I hold it up and I press the button but nothing works sometimes it stays for like two seconds but then it falls down again. *(Ben fools with the umbrella. They all watch. He pulls his hands away. The umbrella stays up. Pause.)*

BEN. Wa-lah. *(Sharon laughs just a couple laughs. No one else laughs.)*

MARY. It's funny, when you first moved in we didn't know if anyone was actually living next door. Ben swore he saw someone coming and going. But at weird times. And the sheets stayed up for so long it still looked empty. It was driving him crazy! So when I saw you yesterday morning I knew I had to grab you. And tell you that we didn't know you were there, that's why we didn't stop by to say hello.

SHARON. We're still not totally moved in. The house belongs to his aunt.

KENNY. Belonged to my aunt. She passed away.

MARY. Oh, that was your aunt?

KENNY. We're renting it for a while before they sell.

SHARON. We'll probably buy it, though.

BEN. That's the way to do it, from a friend or family member. You can avoid a lot of closing costs.

KENNY. That's what they say.

SHARON. So yes, it's a new start! I mean we don't have any furniture even!

MARY. Oh everybody says that, "We don't have any furniture."

KENNY. Well —

BEN. There are some good outlet stores over on 265. That's where I got my TV chair.

MARY. Oh wait I've got something! *(Mary goes inside. She has a little trouble with the sliding glass door. She is just inside the house, so she can call back to the group.)*

SHARON. Such a great back yard.

MARY. *(Calling from inside.)* Isn't it great?

BEN. Thanks, we love it. It sold us on the neighborhood.

SHARON. Hey, who is the woman who jogs around the neighborhood in the hot pink jogging outfit?

MARY. What?

SHARON. Who is the woman who jogs around the neighborhood in the hot pink jogging outfit?

MARY. I don't know. I've never seen her. Ben, have you seen this woman? Jogging?

BEN. No, I don't think so. There are a lot of people jogging in the morning.

SHARON. This one wears a hot pink jogging suit. *(Mary is back at the door, carrying a coffee table, trying to get it through the door.)*

MARY. I don't know. I don't know who that is. Wait, wait let me help. Oh God this door!

KENNY. Hold on, I've got it. I've got it. *(Kenny opens the door. Mary awkwardly carries the coffee table through the door and places it somewhere on the lawn. It is an older model, kind of heavy and clunky, maybe with a glass top. Mary puts the coffee table down in front of Sharon.)*

MARY. This is for you.

SHARON. What?

MARY. You said you didn't have any furniture. So this is for you.

BEN. Honey that's our coffee table.

MARY. I hate this coffee table. Do you like it?

KENNY. Uh yeah it's nice. Do you like it?

MARY. I mean it's a good coffee table, it's very sturdy I think it will be good for you I just —

SHARON. I love it. *(Pause.)* Thank you.

MARY. It's for you.

SHARON. I know. It's amazing. *(Sharon half-touches the coffee table.)*

MARY. Now Ben has to buy me a new table! Ha Ha!

BEN. Ha — Ha. *(Sharon sits and indicates the coffee table to Kenny, like "nice table, right?" Ben speaks kind of loud.)* Alright everybody I'm going to throw these puppies on the grill!

KENNY. *(To Sharon. If Mary hears her, she pretends not to hear it.)* Can you imagine if they really were puppies? *(Sharon and Kenny giggle at their private joke. Mary speaks to Ben.)*

MARY. Did you do the marinade? *(She takes a step and something hurts in her foot.)* OW! *(Sharon half gets up from her chair.)*

SHARON. Are you OK?

MARY. Yes, no, ow, it's fine, I just have this well I have this oh god plantars wart in the bottom of my foot god so embarrassing but do you know what that is? This is a really nasty yes wart that grows upward, INTO your foot, slowly so it takes you a while to notice it, and when you finally do it hurts hurts hurts and you try to put that drugstore wart remover stuff on it and it won't work, and so you go to the doctor — I went to the doctor, I went to the doctor today - and he said he could cut it out but he would have to inject anesthesia into my foot and then do minor surgery — I know —

and since I knew you all were coming over I thought it would be best to wait so I'm having it done next Thursday and just making do until then. It is only when I step a certain way ... it must hit a nerve or something.

KENNY. Like when you have a cavity?

SHARON. Oh right and you bite down on ice or something soft like an apple that goes way up?

KENNY. Or like a caramel candy.

MARY. And start chewing everything super cautiously, like half-chewing because you're afraid of that zap and then one day you forget and you bite regular — *(Everybody kinds of groans and cringes.)*

BEN. OK OK let's not — eew — now you've given me the creeps.

KENNY. Let's talk about something else.

MARY. Yes, let's. Sorry, let's.

BEN. So where do you guys work?

KENNY. I work in a warehouse over off of 694.

SHARON. I work in a phone bank. Is that what you call it? It's like customer service. I sit in one of the booths take the calls and either give people answers or send them on to the supervisor.

MARY. Oh that sounds interesting.

SHARON. Really?

MARY. I work as a paralegal at Furley, Clark and Lamb.

KENNY. What do you do Ben?

BEN. Ha ha I'm a deadbeat. No but really I got laid off my job at this bank, I was a loan officer and they like laid everybody off like literally I don't know who is doing the work anymore and so they gave me this like halfway decent severance pay and also I could get unemployment so I am using it as an opportunity to set up my own business.

MARY. He's home all day.

BEN. It's a financial planning business. Helping people with their credit scores, that sort of thing.

SHARON. Ha we could use that help!

BEN. You and a lot of people, it can slip so fast.

SHARON. And then you can't get it back up again.

BEN. Well, there are strategies, but it takes a lot of patience. We can have a session sometime.

SHARON. That would be great.

BEN. I need to practice on people. You all can be my test case. And then when you're hanging out on your private yacht I can use a quote from you on my website.

SHARON. Sounds good to me!

MARY. He's designing a website. The whole business is going to be run right inside of it.

BEN. I'm building it myself to save money.

MARY. He's got this great book and it talks a lot about breathing deep and taking your time.

SHARON. Uh huh

BEN. And how important it is to spend a lot of time doing things you're passionate about. If you follow your passions, you're halfway there.

MARY. If you panic and start to cut corners, then forget it, it's like building a house on quicksand.

BEN. It's really all about envisioning your life as financially sound.

MARY. It's scary but I really think it's true. It's a great book.

KENNY. Oh so maybe that's why you had that dream?

MARY. Dream?

KENNY. The one about the bank being a card table at the edge of an abandoned whatchamacalit. With the deposits in the shoebox.

MARY. Oh right.

BEN. Alright, we gonna eat some meat! *(Ben gets up to check the meat.)*

SHARON. *(To Ben.)* Are you British?

BEN. What?

SHARON. Are you from England?

BEN. No, why?

SHARON. I don't know. Something about the way you talk. "Now you've given me the creeps."

BEN. "Now you've given me the creeps." I didn't even realize I said it like that. Huh.

SHARON. Maybe you're British.

BEN. *(Kind of laughs but he doesn't really know what she means.)* Yeah, maybe. *(We hear the meat sizzling on the grill.)*

SHARON. Wow steak. *(We hear the grill and some surrounding sounds.)*

BEN. Does anyone want a beer? *(Kenny and Sharon overlap in their reply.)*

KENNY and SHARON. We don't drink. *(Mary speaks under her breath.)*

MARY. I told you that Ben. *(Short pause.)*

BEN. Oh well does anyone need anything? What are you drinking seltzer?

KENNY. I'm OK.

SHARON. I'd love a little more ice.

MARY. Oh I'll bring out a bucket.

BEN. Mary these are just going to be a couple more minutes if you want to check the potatoes.

MARY. Oh right. *(Mary goes inside.)*

KENNY. So this is a nice patio. Was it here when you moved in?

BEN. Yes it was, yeah it's great.

KENNY. I thought maybe you laid it yourself.

BEN. No, no I work in a bank.

KENNY. The edges, the way the cement is pulling up from the edges, it looks like a do it yourself job.

BEN. Really? Is that a problem? I don't / think I noticed —

KENNY. No, no it's totally fine, it's just cosmetic, I only noticed because for a little while I was laying concrete, helping a friend with his business and we did a lot of patios so I learned a lot about it. But it's fine.

BEN. Yeah I never noticed.

KENNY. You have to buy this sealant and put it on at just the right time or the concrete wants to pull away like that. Really though you're fine.

BEN. Maybe you know why our sliding glass door slides so funny.

KENNY. Oh well I —

BEN. See you have to jiggle it like this to get it over the "hump" see? So you start to open it and you have to go — *(He jiggles the door, it opens.)* And then it opens. It isn't a big deal but — *(Kenny squats down and examines the track of the door.)*

KENNY. Oh yeah right look it's the track, I think you might just need a whole new track but later on let me bang on it a bit with a — do you have a rubber mallet?

BEN. No I don't think so.

KENNY. I'll get one. I'll get one and I'll bring it over here and I'll bang on it and we'll see I think I can fix it. *(Mary slides through the door with the ice bucket.)*

MARY. Excuse me.

KENNY. Excuse me.

MARY. The potatoes are perfect!

BEN. Ditto on the steaks! *(Sharon takes some ice and puts it in her*

14

glass and smiles at Mary.)
SHARON. This is awesome. It is so awesome. I mean who invites their neighbors over for dinner anymore?
BEN. Ha we don't have any friends.
MARY. Ben!
BEN. Well.
SHARON. Really though I mean we've lived in a bunch of neighborhoods now — apartments, houses, condos, even a hotel for a little while —
KENNY. The house we were renting had a sewer leak —
MARY. Eew —
SHARON. So the landlord had to put us in a hotel — we've lived in a lot of places and never, never did the neighbors give us the time of day. Neighbors. I mean why is that word still in the dictionary it's archaic am I saying the right word? Because you don't need to talk to your neighbors anymore I mean does anyone borrow a cup of sugar anymore? No you drive to the 24-hour grocery. Because you don't want to bother your neighbors. And so if you come home from work and you do see your neighbor like, getting out of their car or calling their kid inside — wait, what am I saying, kids don't play outside anymore, they might get seduced by some homicidal drug addicts ahhhh! Anyway if you get home and your neighbor is out setting the timer off on their watering system then you look at the ground or maybe give a quick wave and run inside. Because maybe you had a bad day or maybe you have pink eye or something and you don't want to get too close to them. Always an excuse. And when you get inside, behind your closed door, quiet in your house, you make a pact with yourself to talk to them next time but then things get ... fucked up ... oh sorry I didn't mean to say that I apologize —
KENNY. She has a sailor mouth.
SHARON. I do, I'm working on it, but I just think there is no real communication anymore, real communication about real things, about that steak or that sliding glass door or yes I would love some more ice but here we are, having that sort of communication and it's just so ... it's so beautiful — *(Sharon starts to cry. Head in hands. A moment or two of just Sharon crying, like, deep, private weeping. Ben and Mary look for a moment then Ben busies himself at the grill. Kenny gets up.)*
KENNY. It's OK sweetie, just — *(Kenny leans over to comfort Sha-*

ron and WHAM the patio umbrella comes crashing down hitting him on the head.) OW!

BEN. Oh shit. *(Kenny is holding the back of his head.)*

SHARON. Baby are you OK?

KENNY. Yeah, yeah it's just hold on I gotta sit down. Whoo I'm seeing stars.

MARY. Oh wait you're bleeding you're bleeding let me get a towel. *(Mary races inside, she can't get the sliding door open.)*

BEN. You have to jiggle it jiggle it jiggle it no like this — *(Ben runs over and jiggles the door or does Kenny get up and jiggle it with his hand still on his head?)*

KENNY. No it's OK really I'm sure it's just I just need a second — *(He takes his hand away — he really is bleeding.)* Oh wait yeah, maybe a towel.

SHARON. Shit, baby, just keep the pressure on — *(Mary runs back out with a towel.)*

MARY. I can't believe this. Ben, that *(Quickly, almost under her breath —)* Goddamned *(Back to normal voice —)* umbrella!

BEN. I know, I know.

KENNY. It's OK it's gonna be fine —

SHARON. He's got a hard head right baby?

KENNY. Heh-heh. Maybe a little ice?

SHARON. The ice is right here. *(Sharon gets a handful of ice out of the bucket and puts it in the towel.)*

MARY. Ben let's just take the umbrella out, OK? Like I suggested yesterday. Because this keeps happening and I didn't want anyone to get hurt. So let's just take the thirty seconds — *(Ben slips the umbrella out from the hole and leans it against the house.)* Yes the thirty seconds it takes to take the umbrella out so no one gets hurt, and we can consider a new umbrella, that isn't from the fucking — excuse me — bargain basement —

BEN. Mary —

MARY. So that our guests aren't required to get stitches just for daring to come into our back yard.

SHARON. It's OK really —

KENNY. I don't need stitches. I've had stitches before.

BEN. *(Grabbing the umbrella again.)* Where's the tag. I'm calling the manufacturer. In fact I should call them right now — *(Maybe Sharon and Kenny are like no no no no no don't worry, really —)* Kenny we can take you to the hospital. *(Sharon and Kenny are even more like no no no really.)* Where is that tag — *(Ben realizes something about the situation. He slips outside of his tizzy and returns to calm host mode.)* OK. OK look at us. Look at us. Kenny you're fine?

KENNY. Totally. I'm just going to keep the pressure on for a bit.

BEN. Alright, then.

SHARON. *(In a bad British accent.)* "Alrighty, then, Ben."

BEN. What?

SHARON. I said "Alrighty ole chap, cup a tea!" You're British! Admit it! Admit it!

KENNY. Sharon —

BEN. So. How 'bout some steak?

SHARON. Let's do it! *(Ben starts taking steaks off the grill.)*

BEN. Kenny you get the first one in honor of your concussion.

KENNY. Ha Ha.

MARY. Potatoes.

SHARON. Do you all ever have "twice baked" potatoes.

BEN. Oh yeah with all that cream in them.

SHARON. Yes!

MARY. Sometimes but they are so much work.

SHARON. My mom used to make those all the time. *(A few moments of sitting down and settling in. Ben is sitting down and they are all taking their first bites.)*

KENNY. Aw yeah. *(Kenny gives Ben the thumbs up.)*

MARY. Delicious honey. *(Does one of them get a piece of gristle and do that weird chewing thing where you have to get it out of your mouth and spit it in your napkin? Ben glances over into Kenny and Sharon's yard.)*

SHARON. I can't believe I cried.

MARY. Oh, now —

BEN. Cried?

SHARON. A few minutes ago. When I was talking about neighbors.

BEN. God did I miss that? Did I forget?

SHARON. They say it's part of the process, feeling things, letting your emotions just happen, in real time, rather than running away from them on that glossy motorcade of substances.

MARY. Process?

KENNY. *(Under his breath.)* Baby we were going to keep that / to ourselves —

SHARON. Kenny and I met in Eldridge Smith Tomforde.

MARY. *(Gets it.)* Oh. *(Ben is eating.)*

BEN. *(Chipper, Oblivious.)* What's Eldridge Smith Tomforde?

(Pause for a moment.)

MARY. It's a rehab facility, honey. For substance abuse.

BEN. *(Still Chipper.)* Oh so that's why you don't drink.

KENNY. Yes and that's why we don't smoke crack or shoot meth or snort big fat lines of cocaine at four in the morning for the third day in a row. *(Quick pause then Sharon starts to laugh. Then Kenny laughs and Mary sort of smiles. Mary stays really quiet during this next section.)*

BEN. Well, more power to you. And so you met in this … this …

SHARON. Facility. Yes we were both in for three months — we arrived the same week.

KENNY. And we resisted the attraction for at least a month.

SHARON. Because you're supposed to. You're actually supposed to resist it for a year but —

KENNY. *(Re: Hot Sharon.)* But who can resist this right? *(Ben and Kenny laugh knowingly but it is a little weird.)*

SHARON. And it's so strange "getting out." Those doors part and you walk outside into the hot air, thinking about your apartment that's waiting for you, still sealed shut, filled with all your crappy stuff, dishes molding in the sink, countertops piled with old beer cans and underwear and pipes and stuffed animals covered in puke. And you're standing outside the hospital, clutching each other's sweaty hands for dear life — And then there was this house.

KENNY. My aunt died.

SHARON. There was this house, and — this is not a lie — we went to TJ Maxx, and I bought a dress with flowers on it, and a pair of "flats." "Flats" and Kenny bought a suit —

KENNY. It was $250 marked down to $34.99.

SHARON. And he bought shoes also, and an undershirt and socks …

KENNY. And we went to see my great-uncle, who was very close to my aunt — she left the house to him —

SHARON. And we asked if we could live here. We asked him to give us a chance. *(Blackout. The sounds of the neighborhood moving into night: The hum of air conditioning units, and air conditioning units starting up and shutting off, a couple cars driving by, a car or two parking, doors opening and closing. Perhaps an automatic garage door opening? The faint sound of a few joggers jogging, and a few kids riding their bikes. The car and people sounds begin to fade and are replaced by crickets and maybe a few frogs, still mixed in with the air conditioning sounds. And someone is having a fight behind closed doors. Then*

18

the sound of "No, No, No, No, NO" as a door opens and the No's become louder. The same door slams. Loud knocking on another door. A knocking and then the sound of Mary yelling, "Sharon! Sharon open up! Shaaaaron!" And more knocking. Lights up, middle-of-the-night outdoor light. We are in Kenny and Sharon's front yard. Theirs is a very basic brick suburban house. Or maybe siding. Some shrubs but no flowers. Really bare bones. There is one taller potted plant on the porch, a plant that is like a small tree, with some blossoms on it. Other than that, nada. Do we see Mary sneaking out of her back yard in her bathrobe, looking back to see if she is being followed? Or is Mary already at Sharon and Kenny's doorstep when the lights come up, banging on their door? Sharon opens the door in her T-shirt and underwear.) Mary what's — *(Mary falls into her arms. She weeps outright for maybe five seconds —)* Mary can you just — *(Another wave of weeping. Eventually Mary half composes herself. Anytime Mary curses she says that word kind of under her breath.)*

MARY. It's just I don't know how to help him. I'm at the frayed edge of my wits. He gets to be home all day and I don't get home until 6:45 because of the *fucking* traffic on 694 and he's been home all day and I get home and he's already on his first drink. He *says* it's his first drink anyway. And he's cooked dinner which is of course very sweet but then I say something about how his green beans taste different from my green beans you know like, "Oh these taste different," just like that, not saying anything bad but he drops his fork and I know he's offended and then it starts. And I hate "NASCAR Unmasked and Personal" and he knows I hate it I mean he's not a NASCAR kind of guy he doesn't like NASCAR he just likes that show, and he turns it on anyway while I'm finishing my dinner, while I'm washing the dishes and he watches the TV so fucking loud even the commercials and he laughs at commercials, at *dumbfuck* commercials like the one with the cartoon chicken getting rubbed down with chicken magic. *(Mary imitates the commercial. It is a Latino Chicken.)* "Ieeee! It tickles!" I mean Sharon it's so *fucking crackass* dumb. He says it helps him decompress, he's at the computer all day long. And I'm like "doing what? Looking at one of those titty websites? Live chatting with some stripper? How long can a making a WEBSITE possibly take?" No. No I don't say that. I just think it. What I say is: "So how was your day? Did you bring the files to Kinkos" And he's like "No I forgot oh well I'll do it tomorrow" and I say "You know you can do it on their website through the file uploader, it's super easy." And he says "Yes YES I know" and I say "well you know that book you bought for $65.00 said you've got to be hard on yourself about keeping to a schedule. Because Joe Blow down the street is also probably laid off, and also probably about to set up his dream business where you get to sit home all day and tell other people how to clean up the fucking financial wasteland of their day-to-day existence. And if Joe Blow gets his portfolio together before you do then Joe Blow gets the clients, not you." And he's says "Joe Blow can suck my *nutsack.*" *(Pause for a moment, that word is like a bad taste in her mouth.)* And I say "Oh that's a winning attitude." And then that's it — we're fighting and he's all "I'm trying to be proactive" and I'm all "Today sucked, I barely got to eat lunch" and he's all "I'm afraid" and I'm like "Don't say it like that" and he's like "Look I have to put my beer on the floor! The photo album too!" And I'm like "That coffee table didn't GO in this ROOM —

SHARON. You can have it / back —

MARY. I don't want it back.

I want to live in a tent in the woods. With one pot and one pan. And an old fashioned aluminum mess kit with its own mesh bag. I want my hair to smell like the smoke from yesterday's fire, when I cooked my fish and my little white potatoes. I want to dry out my underwear on a warm rock. And feel the cold water rushing around my ankles, my feet pressing into the tiny stone bed that holds up the stream. Silver guppies nosing their heads into my calves … *(Quiet for a moment. We hear suburban wind, maybe a car passing on another street. Maybe some teenagers laughing, maybe some kid in the house across the street listen to music in their room.)*

SHARON. Were you a Girl Scout?

MARY. Yes.

SHARON. I thought so. *(Mary leans over into the bushes, she doesn't get up, she just leans over, and pukes. And pukes. And sits back up.)*

MARY. Oh god, my head. I think I need some water.

SHARON. Mary, have you ever thought about getting some help?

MARY. Some help with what?

SHARON. With your drinking problem. *(Mary looks at Sharon like she is an alien from another planet.)*

MARY. I thought I could just come to you and talk.

SHARON. You can, you did.

MARY. Because you cried at   SHARON. I know.

my house and I thought that
was awesome that you felt
comfortable enough to do
that it made me feel like a
good host that you felt
OK letting go in that way —

SHARON. You are a good host. But you can be a great host and still have a drinking problem. *(Mary gets loud. Too loud for this neighborhood. She no longer quiets her curse words.)*

MARY. You know what FUCK YOU. *(She stands up and stumbles a little.)* I come over here asking for HELP and what is the FIRST THING YOU FUCKING DO? Accuse me of being a fucking DRUNK? I MEAN IF THAT IS NOT THE BLACK CALLING THE KETTLE POT. God. My husband is offering the two of you his services FOR FREE. He wouldn't even blink to ask for payment. Wouldn't even BLINK. And look at you. This fucking yard. *(Ben walks up, he is obviously not drunk; he is stone cold sober and it takes Mary a little while to see him.)* There's not even a single FERN. You've made no effort.

SHARON. Well we just moved in — *(Maybe Mary grabs on to Sharon?)*

MARY. I was hiding behind our bushes. I snuck out the door to get some air. I JUST NEEDED SOME AIR, I needed to get out of the house. And he wouldn't let me. He kept locking the door on me. And so when the commercial came on I snuck out the back and climbed over the fence and just squatted there behind the bushes. He called and called. My toes were in the mulch, I was breathing, I was not answering. Because he doesn't like me, nobody likes me, and I just wanted to breathe. And then I thought Sharon likes me. She cried in my yard. *(Mary pukes over Sharon's shoulder, she has to kind of brush it off her back and the back of her arm. Ben catches Mary. Kenny opens the door, half asleep, in his boxers. Mary realizes that it is Ben who has grabbed her.)* GET AWAY FROM ME GET HIM AWAY! *(Ben pulls Mary to him and speaks softly in her ear. She's listening. She's saying these words as he whispers in her ear.)* Uh-huh. Uh huh. My head is pounding. It's like there's cats inside. I know. I know I'm a good person. I know tootsie too. Yes. Yes. I want to go home. I want to get in the tub. Ow, my foot. *(Mary is quiet in Ben's arms. Ben looks at Sharon and Kenny. Everyone except Mary sees someone approaching. Ben tries to hold Mary up a little better. We hear the sound of footsteps jogging by. All at once Ben, Sharon and Kenny give a quick wave, like they are waving back to someone.)*

BEN. That's her?

SHARON. That's her. How dumb is that, jogging at eleven at night.

KENNY. And she'll be back at it at six-thirty.

SHARON. Showoff.

KENNY. I really need to start exercising again. *(Pause for a quick moment as they watch her go.)*

BEN. I'm really —

SHARON and KENNY. No, really, it's OK really.

BEN. We'll buy you a new shirt -

KENNY. Don't worry, please —

SHARON. We've been through this —

KENNY. Remember?

BEN. I'll see you tomorrow Kenny.

KENNY. One-thirty! *(Ben starts to walk Mary home.)*

BEN. Please don't worry about your yard — *(Mary's foot hurts as she walks.)*

MARY. Ow. OW.

BEN. It's going to be a nice yard. I like that new plant. *(Ben and Mary are almost to their house. Sharon says softly.)*

SHARON. The funny thing is it's fake. *(Sharon and Kenny watch them go for a few seconds. A quick kiss then they head back inside. Before the door closes — Blackout. Daytime sounds. Lawnmowers, kids on bikes, a plane overhead, hum of air conditioner compressors in people's back yards, a couple of birds. Lights up on Mary and Ben's back yard. Ben is at the grill, cleaning it off with a wire brush, turning on the gas. Mary comes out of the house with a lacy tablecloth. We see her foot is bandaged and she is wearing a funny orthopedic sandal on that foot that doesn't let you put pressure on the front of your foot. Ben crosses around the table into the house — he's on a mission. She unfolds the tablecloth, snaps it out and lets it settle into place on the table. Perfect. Mary heads inside and she and Ben cross as he comes out with a tray of chicken covered in Saran Wrap.)*

BEN. Excuse me.

MARY. Excuse me. *(Ben puts the chicken on the tray next to the grill. Mary comes out with a bouquet of fresh flowers, and a candle. Ben checks one last thing, then watches Mary arrange the flowers. Mary lights the candle, and looks at Ben. Are Mary and Ben about to say something nice and/or real to each other? Kenny and Sharon call from inside Ben and Mary's house.)*

SHARON. Hello-oo! Anybody home?

BEN. Come on in,   MARY.
we're in the back!   Eek! Just a second!

(Mary rushes into the house. Perhaps we hear her say something like "Go ahead out, go, go ..." Kenny appears, carrying a two-liter of Dr Pepper, followed by Sharon.)

BEN. Hi!

SHARON. Oh my god this looks amazing!

MARY. *(From inside.)* It's a lawn party! Hold on!

KENNY. We brought this. *(Kenny hands Ben the Dr. Pepper. Sharon admires the flowers.)*

BEN. Thanks — *(Ben puts the Dr Pepper on the table or whatever.)*

SHARON. Oh my god are these real? *(Ben points towards Kenny and Sharon's back yard.)*

BEN. Hey Kenny are you building a deck?

KENNY. Yeah I'm getting started. That's the foundation you see right there, and the boards for the decking. I can't decide if I want to put up a railing or not.

BEN. Well it's nice for leaning —

KENNY. Yeah but then you have to really reinforce it.

BEN. Or for kids, if you want to put kids on the deck —

KENNY. Yeah, well, we're just taking things one step at a time.

BEN. Oh, yeah, sure, of course, I mean really, yeah, us too, right? I mean, I don't know what I'm talking about, I don't even know what end of the hammer to hold.

SHARON. Yeah but you've got smarts Ben. Kenny could never start his own business.

BEN. Who knows! Kenny's got big plans right Kenny? *(Kenny makes some awkward "you got it, Ben" kind of gesture.)*

SHARON. You look like a smart person, Ben.

BEN. Ha, really?

SHARON. Yes, like you should be wearing skinny little suspenders.

MARY. *(Offstage in the house.)* Honey, will you get the door? *(Ben slides the sliding door open for Mary.)* Look how that sliding door just zips open!

BEN. Your husband's a genius, Sharon. *(Kenny smiles. Mary enters with an enormous tray of hors d'oeuvres, beautifully presented. It is a little intimidating how beautifully presented they are.)*

23

MARY. Alright, everybody so we've got some dates wrapped in bacon drizzled with some chili oil and this is a Danish Havarti that I mashed with some basil and it is really great with this special olive oil — you just need a little. These are slices of "heirloom tomatoes" do you know what that is? I drove all the way to Whole Foods to get them. They've been grown from the same seed for hundreds of years, meaning the plants grow and drop their seeds and those seeds are used for the next plants. Try that with the olive oil and a little bit of this special pink salt —

KENNY. Special salt?

MARY. I know, I know, you think "salt," "salt is salt" right? But here taste it with a tomato —

KENNY. Oh I don't like tomatoes —

SHARON. *(As in: be polite.)* Kenny —

MARY. Oh well taste it with the Havarti then. Go ahead taste it — *(She hands him a cracker with havarti and a bit of salt. They watch him taste it. He chews.)*

KENNY. Oh yeah.

MARY. See? I was right, right?

KENNY. Yeah it takes a second but then — wow! Taste this.

SHARON. I wish I could cook. *(He feeds a bite to Sharon.)*

MARY. Oh you can cook! It's special pink salt from the bottom of a special river. Ben, what's the name of that river? Ben? And this — *(She holds up a little bowl.)* Is caviar.

BEN. Caviar?

MARY. Caviar that came all the way from Norway.

SHARON. Wow. Kenny won't even let me buy Dijon mustard. *(Mary hands Sharon some caviar on a cracker.)*

BEN. Where did you buy caviar?

MARY. It doesn't matter Ben.

SHARON. Oh it's good!

MARY. Right? *(Ben claps his hands.)*

BEN. OK let's throw these puppies on the grill!

MARY. Oh Ben let's wait just a few minutes. I just brought out the appetizers.

BEN. Yes but chicken takes longer.

MARY. Let's sit a minute — *(Mary pulls a patio chair so it is side by side with hers.)*

BEN. But I —

MARY. I know but let's just relax a minute.

KENNY. Come sit, Ben.

SHARON. Rest. *(Tiny pause.)*

BEN. OK, alright. *(Ben sits next to Mary. Mary grabs his hand and holds it. Smile. Pause. Sharon sings a line from an early '80s pop song to them, getting the words a bit wrong.*)*

BEN. Oh I love that song.

KENNY. Remember MTV?

SHARON. It's still on, dummy. *(Ben sings the next line of the chorus of the song to Sharon, getting the words wrong.)*

MARY. What about you Sharon how's work?

SHARON. Oh, you know —

MARY. Sure and you Kenny?

KENNY. You know it's a job.

BEN. You've just got to reach the one-year mark.

KENNY. One solid year with the same job and same address. Then everything starts to open up —

MARY. Like a good bottle of wine.

BEN. *(To Sharon.)* We had a great session.

SHARON. He told me. So Ben is it true you're a NASCAR man? *(Ben laughs.)*

BEN. No, no. I just like the show, that behind-the-scenes show. It's just brain drain you know. The drivers and their trophies. And their trophy wives. A good way to decompress. I barely have to pay attention.

MARY. One time I watched a whole episode of "Fit to Be Tied" and when it got to the end, I realized that I hadn't really seen any of it.

SHARON. Yes!

MARY. I was stewing about something else the whole time ... to Ben it looked like I was watching the show, but really I was on another planet ... a really angry planet.

KENNY. That sounds like the last five years of my life.

SHARON. Up until now, right?

KENNY. Sure thing, hotpants.

BEN. *(Laughing a little.)* Hotpants —

SHARON. I'm going to try meditation

BEN. Really. *(Kenny is kind of cracking up. Sharon hits his leg while she speaks.)*

SHARON. So I can stay in the moment. I'm going to start with ten minutes a day, just breathing in and out through my nose, fac-

---

* See Addendum for information on possible song lyrics.

ing the wall.

KENNY. You can't sit still for ten seconds!

BEN. Sometimes I look up from my computer and three hours have passed, like THAT. *(Ben snaps.)*

SHARON. See! If you meditated, you could have those three hours back.

KENNY. It doesn't work that way, baby.

MARY. Oh my god he gets so zoned into that computer you would swear he was looking at porn.

BEN. Mary —

MARY. Don't worry I checked your search history once. It was all mortgage rates and motivational websites — and one random site about mining rocks and minerals! *(Mary makes a face like "Wha? What is that about!" Mary and Sharon laugh. Does Ben sort of half-laugh and shrug?)*

BEN. I was just curious …

KENNY. *(To Ben, but everyone can hear, regarding his search history.)* Dude you can clear that shit. Then you can go anywhere you want.

BEN. I think I'll put the meat on. *(Ben gets up to tend to the meat.)*

KENNY. Hey Mary how's your foot?

MARY. Oh it's good. The thing took like 20 minutes. The worst part was the shot. The doctor stuck the needle into the arch of my foot and I could feel it shoot all the way up, through my stomach and heart and throat and into my eyeball.

BEN. I've never heard her yell like that.

MARY. But then everything went dead and the doctor could just dig right in.

KENNY. Eew. It didn't hurt?

MARY. This shoe hurts more than the operation, actually, but they say I have to wear it.

KENNY. *(To Mary.)* I'm glad you're feeling better.

SHARON. See Mary went to the doctor it was *fine.* Kenny's afraid of the doctor.

KENNY. I'm working on it.

BEN. All I want in the whole world is a meat thermometer. Mary can we get a meat thermometer?

MARY. Kenny do you want to try some caviar?

KENNY. The funny thing is I'm allergic.

MARY. To caviar?

SHARON. He puffs up instantly. We were in the VIP section in this club in Atlanta, and they had all this fancy shit. Excuse me this fancy food. And we were well we were high as kites and just eating and eating and all of a sudden he was on the floor, his eyes turning black, his whole face getting puffier and puffier.

KENNY. I couldn't breathe.

SHARON. They called an ambulance.

KENNY. Which sucked because I didn't have insurance.

SHARON. Three days in the hospital. I slept there. He woke up with night sweats. The doctor said if I ever eat caviar I should brush my teeth because if I kiss him, especially if I tongue kiss him, he could just blow up again. Like a blowfish. He's that allergic.

KENNY. It was crazy. That was like eight years ago. I've avoided caviar ever since.

MARY. But wait I thought you met in rehab?

KENNY. Oh that's a funny story.

MARY. What do you mean?

SHARON. We did meet in rehab but we just realized a couple weeks ago that we had met before. In Hotlanta. And we had that adventure together. I actually snuck out of the hospital while he was asleep and got on a bus to Chi-town. Chicago. I mean I hardly knew him then. I mean we were a mess.

KENNY. I think we both just erased Hotlanta from our minds. What was the name of that club?

SHARON. Who knows. Razoo. Numbers. Buzz Buzz.

KENNY. The Compound. Third Base.

SHARON. Ampersand.

KENNY. Pirate Dan's. *(Sharon kind of chuckles a bit. Kenny does too. It's a private moment, a mutual acknowledgment that "Hotlanta was fucked up, yo." Mary picks up a pitcher.)*

MARY. Lemon ginger iced tea?

SHARON. Why thank you, I would love some lemon ginger iced tea.

BEN. *(Trying his best to focus on the meat.)* OK. I think this will be about fifteen more minutes. Do you two like asparagus?

SHARON. I adore asparagus.

KENNY. *(Like, what you crazy bitch?)* What?

SHARON. *(At Kenny, perturbed.)* You don't eat vegetables.

BEN. Neither does Mary.

MARY. I eat potatoes.

BEN and KENNY. That doesn't count. *(They all kind of chuckle that they said that together.)*

KENNY. Because that would make French fries count, right Mary? I love me some French fries.

MARY. Me too. *(Mary kind of blushes as she eats a date wrapped in bacon.)*

SHARON. You guys have to come over. Soon. I mean look at that, the yard is right there. I could spit and hit it. Watch I'm going to spit. *(Sharon spits and hits the yard.)*

KENNY. Yes let's make that happen. As soon as the deck is finished.

SHARON. Fuck the deck! Oh, sorry. I mean fart on the deck! These are our neighbors, Kenny. We've lived here almost five weeks. We've got to have our neighbors over. We've got to fight against the anonimater … anonyminimous …

MARY and BEN. *(Staggered, trying to help her with the word.)* Anonymity?

SHARON. Yes! We've got to fight that. I mean everywhere else we lived we hid from our neighbors and they hid from us because nobody wanted to interact with us EVER, I mean they knew, they could see. And they could just ignore us la la la la la — that's your space, this is mine, no I don't hear the screams and moans of a drug addict no I don't see those junkie friends with blood caked in their hair la la that's your space. Dust your hands, shoot the rooster in the foot and be done with it. But things are different now. We can have company. We can have a nice time.

MARY. Of course you can.

SHARON. Tomorrow. Come over tomorrow.

KENNY. Sharon there's nowhere to sit!

SHARON. We'll figure it out. Mary and Ben, would you like to come to our house for dinner tomorrow?

KENNY. It's not our house.

SHARON. Shut up. Will you? Come over? Will you let us make you dinner at our place? Tomorrow? *(Ben sings the line from the pop song once again, again getting it wrong.)*

MARY. Ben. I mean Ben do we have plans?

BEN. Sure, I mean no. No plans.

MARY. That would be lovely. *(Sharon is excited but also kind of freaked out, as she really does not have the skills or money to pull this sort of thing off.)*

SHARON. Awesome. Great. Fun. Alright. Dinner at our place. Fantastic. *(Sharon spins around in one circle.)* Really, super fun! *(Blackout. Outdoor sounds again, the next day. When the lights come up, we are in Kenny and Sharon's back yard. The deck Kenny has started building is half finished: the floor is only 3/4 put down and most of the boards are loose. Ben and Mary sit in super crappy folding chairs that really look second hand — maybe Sharon and Kenny got them out of the basement. There is also an old-fashioned card table with one joint taped up with duct tape. Sharon is sitting on a plastic milk crate, upturned. Maybe Kenny will sit on a couple bags of charcoal? Oh or maybe a suitcase? The grill is from the Dollar General. There is a plastic pot of plastic flowers on the card table. Kenny is working the grill. Sharon relates a dream.)* And I was wandering around inside this strange house. But I knew the house was inside of another house. A house inside a house. I could feel the two houses. And there were these rubber walls, you could press your hand right into them. And I was walking through the house and thinking "I've got to get this caviar to Mary" *(Mary laughs.)* But I knew that Kenny was allergic to caviar and so I didn't want to touch it, so I built this contraption out of chopsticks? To carry the caviar and I hooked it around my waist right — *(She indicates her abdomen.)*

MARY. Oh my god do you think you're pregnant?

SHARON. NO. Definitely no. God no. So I opened this door in the hallway and inside on this fancy bed was the lady in the pink jogging suit getting the shit fucked out of her /by some guy —

KENNY. Sharon! *(Sharon lifts her hand to her mouth quickly.)*

SHARON. Oh god. Shit I didn't mean that.

BEN. Well, that's what was happening. In the dream.

SHARON. Can I finish it? The dream? *(Ben and Mary are like "sure, sure.")* So I closed the door on her and then I was in the supermarket, the one I used to go to when I was a kid. And I was with Ben but Ben wasn't Ben. He was this short guy, maybe five-feet tall, with this really bad brown dye job on his hair and his beard, and he may have been a leprechaun, but I knew it was Ben and I knew he was STARVING and I had to buy him food. And I would put food in the cart and check my purse for money but the amount of money I had kept changing, so I would put back the tomatoes and put in maybe green beans because they were cheaper and I would check my purse and not have enough money and put stuff back, and so on and so on — And I knew I had to feed Ben, he was shriveling, getting smaller, he was sitting in the child's seat of the shopping cart by then. And then we were at the butcher counter and I picked Ben up and went behind the counter into the meat locker back there. I sat Ben down on an icy side of beef and he smiled at me and the butcher came by, looked in, and closed the door right on us. It was cold and I could feel the frost on my face. I tried to form words — I tried to say, "Ben, Ben get the door open, we're going to die!" But it just came out like — "Buuuh — Buuuh" and then Ben scratched his little beard and put his hand on my hand and I got this intense wave of peace. Radiating through me, like when a tab of ecstasy hits, and I thought "Oh, I'm dying" but it was so amazing, this feeling of sadness and happiness coming from inside and radiating out, like what bleeding to death must feel like, and then Ben said, in a British accent: *(Ben speaks in a British accent. It's a pretty good one. Does he touch Sharon's hand as well?)*

BEN. When I look at you, I see nothing but becoming. *(Mary kind of freezes.)*

MARY. Wha — *(Sharon smiles. Mary is a little freaked.)* I — I — I think I'm —

BEN. *(Still in a British accent?.)* Well, I was in the dream wasn't I? *(Short pause. Then Ben and Sharon start laughing.)*

SHARON. No, no I already told him the dream —

MARY. Oh.

BEN. She told me before you came over.

KENNY. That was a good accent, Ben!

BEN. *(In a British accent.)* Not bad there chap, eh?

SHARON. See? It's in there somewhere … *(Does Sharon kind of tickle Ben like the Pillsbury doughboy?)*

MARY. That was … weird …

SHARON. That was my dream. And I think it was my closure dream. I think I'm better now. Kenny, I'm completely healed.

MARY. I'm going inside. Sharon did you put the vodka inside?

SHARON. It's on the counter.

MARY. And may I use your bathroom?

SHARON. Sure, you'll see it. Right there in the hallway. *(Mary goes inside Kenny and Sharon's house. Kenny claps his hands together.)*

KENNY. Alright let's throw these puppies on the grill!

SHARON. Hey Ben I figured out the other day that all the streets around here are named for different kinds of light. We're on "Sunshine Way" and then there's "Ultraviolet Lane," "Fluorescent Avenue."

KENNY. Also Rainbow Road.

BEN. Yes, AND did you also notice "Feather Way" ... "Weightless Avenue" ...

KENNY. *(Getting it.)* Oooh, right — Helium Street ...

SHARON. Uhhhh ...

BEN. "Light" and "light." *(Sharon gets it.)*

SHARON. Oooooooh!

KENNY. Weird right?

SHARON. Totally weird.

BEN. They planned it that way back in the '60s. If you go to the corner of Sunshine and Route 20, there is this big brick sign that fell backwards a long time ago ... twenty years ago? It's all overgrown with weeds and ivy. But if you peel some of it away you can see the original engraved sign "Bright Houses. Come to the Light"

KENNY. How'd you find that?

BEN. I had a friend who lived here in high school. We were just messing around.

KENNY. It's still there?

BEN. I think so. *(Weird beat. Will the conversation shift? Sharon panics.)*

SHARON. OH SHIT! I forgot the appetizers!

BEN. That's OK.

SHARON. No they're just inside. I'll be right back. *(Sharon goes inside. Ben goes up to the deck, kind of "testing" it.)*

KENNY. Hey, man thanks again for all the advice.

BEN. Oh, it's not me, it's the book.

KENNY. Yeah but I never would have read that book.

BEN. I'm glad it helped. The deck's sure coming along.

KENNY. Yeah it's gonna be nice. We should sit down again sometime soon.

BEN. Sure thing. *(Ben looks at the grill)* What is it burgers?

KENNY. Yes with a ball of American cheese inside. It melts while it cooks.

BEN. *(As in, shit yeah.)* Yeah.

KENNY. You have to be careful though you'll burn your mouth. Hold on I need some salt. *(Kenny moves towards the house.)* You need anything?

BEN. Maybe another beer.

KENNY. You got it. *(Kenny goes inside as Mary comes outside. She has a very big plastic cup of vodka tonic. Mary goes to Ben, speaking with her voice a little hushed.)*

31

MARY. Ben, there's nothing in there.

BEN. What?

MARY. They've lived here five weeks. And there is no furniture in there. Nothing. Except the coffee table we gave them and this one arm chair with stuffing coming out of it. It looks like a dog ate it. And a tiny TV sitting on a cardboard box ...

BEN. Well they said they had no furniture.

MARY. Yes, but NO FURNITURE.

BEN. They're starting from scratch.

MARY. And I think there is a smell. Like a bad carpet smell. Like a sick carpet smell.

BEN. Oh come on.

MARY. Even the bedroom — *(Mary takes a big gulp of vodka tonic.)*

BEN. You went in their bedroom?

MARY. There's not even a bed. I mean there is this mattress looking thing, and some sheets barely hanging off it, onto the floor, and that TJ Maxx suit hanging like a carcass in the closet.

BEN. You looked in the closet?

MARY. I don't know it just makes me feel strange, I mean who are we talking to?

BEN. They're getting it together. I'm sure they have no credit cards, no nothing. I don't even know how he bought this lumber.

MARY. They did buy curtains.

BEN. Only for the front, did you notice?

MARY. Well. They're trying to be good neighbors, I guess. *(Mary and Ben look at each other and breathe one breath. What have they gotten themselves into? No, Ben thinks it's awesome, dammit.)*

BEN. I don't know, I think they're great.

MARY. No furniture, no clothes.

BEN. Mary will you just shut up about it? You're being judgmental. Kenny's got a good game plan.

MARY. Well, you're the expert.

BEN. How much vodka is in there?

MARY. It's not yours.

BEN. I can smell it over here.

MARY. It's just strange. I feel strange. *(Kenny enters.)*

KENNY. Ladies and gentlemen, drumroll please! *(Kenny holds the door open. Sharon enters with a rusty cookie sheet with some snacks on it.)*

SHARON. Alright so you all the theme is white trash because I'm trying to own up to what I am these days ha ha and anyway the Cheetos are always the first things to go at a party right? Even when they're sitting right next to the brie. SO, we've got Cheetos, Saltines, a canned bean dip and Cheez Whiz, and then I made Delta Caviar, ha ha no really it's like anti-caviar so we don't kill Kenny. It's got a can of corn, red peppers and yellow peppers, a can of black-eyed peas and some Italian dressing, and salt. At least we can afford salt! Wait till you taste it!

BEN. I have a weakness for the bean dip. *(Ben digs in.)*

SHARON. Mary try some.

MARY. I'll have a Cheeto. *(Mary takes one Cheeto. Kenny returns with Ben's beer and goes to the grill.)*

BEN. God it's so nice to just chill out like this. When I started working from home I imagined myself totally relaxed, working a couple hours, going for a jog, doing a little gardening —

MARY. You don't garden —

BEN. I know I just imagined it. But instead my days are so hectic. I'm always on the phone or learning more HTML for my website —

SHARON. Ha ask Kenny about trying to learn HTML —

KENNY. HTML can kiss my sweet ripe ass —

BEN. Running to Staples Jesus Christ how many times a day can a man go to Staples! Anyway I am totally fried by the time Mary comes home and kind of panicky because I feel like I didn't get enough done.

KENNY. When do you "launch"?

BEN. Well it was supposed to be this past Monday. But everything always takes longer than you think.

MARY. I still don't understand how JUST A WEBSITE is going to attract customers. I mean it is just hanging out there in the ether. Is someone just going to decide they need a consultant and then POOF find your website?

BEN. I've got it baby —

MARY. No I just mean there are like what, a gazillion bazillion websites out there —

BEN. I've got it.

SHARON. Anyway I heard the "next internet" is coming out soon. Something that we can't even imagine. This super fast thing that will change everything. Change everything so much that like we won't even have to own things anymore. Because the whole thing will become obsolete. Like landlines.

BEN. Do you mean — I don't understand. I mean what will happen to websites. I don't understand.

SHARON. That's just it, I can't explain it, and it's outside of our understanding at this time —

BEN. I mean I'm sure there'll be some sort of conversion, a way to convert the website into —

SHARON. Ben. No worries. Our tiny brains can't conceive of it, it's totally new, like finding out ... this table is actually alive, and has been for a long time. We can't understand it yet, but the inventors of the "next internet" are doing that part for us. So you, Ben, should just unfurrow — is that a word? Unfurrow that forehead and enjoy some bean dip and Delta Caviar. *(The distant sound of Sharon and Kenny's doorbell. Sharon looks puzzled.)* Is that our doorbell? *(Everyone pauses, listens, ambient sounds of the neighborhood. Are they the same as usual or have they changed? A moment. Another moment. Another doorbell.)*

MARY. I think it is.

SHARON. Who on earth can be ringing our doorbell?

KENNY. Do you want me to get it?

SHARON. No you finish the burgers. *(Sharon exits.)*

KENNY. Okay, two minutes. *(Kenny explodes, weirdly, yelling to Sharon way too loudly for a simple condiment request.)* HEY SHARON WHEN YOU COME OUT BRING THE BUNS AND THE KETCHUP AND STUFF! She also made potato salad. She makes awesome potato salad.

MARY. I wonder why it was a meat locker.

KENNY. What?

MARY. In the dream.

KENNY. Oh. Who knows.

MARY. Do you dream, Kenny? *(Kenny laughs, maybe for a long time, then shuts down this conversation.)*

KENNY. No. *(Kenny turns back to the grill. Mary might say the next line in a British accent.)*

MARY. Ben would you get me another drink?

BEN. No. *(Mary kind of pouts.)* I'll get you 7UP. I'll get you 7UP if you want it. Mary, will you please let me get you a 7UP? *(Mary kind of clicks her tongue and sighs.)*

MARY. Sure, alright. *(She hands Ben her cup. Ben gets up and starts to go towards the house.)*

KENNY. Hey Mary, Sharon was asking about those plastic plates you have — *(Suddenly Ben falls through one of the boards of the porch. Either it breaks or there was like a slot that his foot could slide through. He falls one or two feet into the porch and catches himself with his hand.)*

BEN. SHIT!

KENNY. Oh god — *(Kenny goes to help him.)*

BEN. Ow ow ow SHIT!

MARY. Is it broken?

BEN. The porch?

MARY. No your leg, you *fucking* imbecile.

KENNY. Let me help you.

BEN. I think it's bleeding, ow OW wait take it slow shit … Ahhh … *(Ben is now sitting on the porch, his leg has a deep scratch or gash from the wood.)*

KENNY. I'm getting some ice, and water, don't move. Are you sure it's not broken?

BEN. No, no I don't think so. *(Kenny runs inside.)*

MARY. *Fuckwad.*

BEN. MARY! It's not me, it's the PORCH!

MARY. That new internet is going to come and then where will we be? *(Kenny comes running out with a cup of water and some ice and a paper towel.)*

KENNY. Man, this was totally my fault man, SHIT hold on let's pour some water in it, to clean it out — *(Kenny pours water on the wound, It HURTS.)*

BEN. Ow Ow! This is so dumb!

KENNY. I think there are splinters in there. I think we need to pull them out with a tweezer.

BEN. Give me a second, man. Just give me a second.

KENNY. Aw Man do you have insurance?

MARY. Maybe hydrogen peroxide.

BEN. Just give me a second. *(We hear Sharon yelling at someone from inside the house.)*

SHARON. Yeah you too you fucking nutcase! You're a fucking stinky cunt, you hear me? You are insane! *(Sharon enters carrying buns, a bottle of ketchup, a jar of mustard and a jar of hamburger dill slices. It is a little awkward. Oh and also she is furious. At some point during this tirade Mary slips in the house for some more vodka. Also at some point Sharon puts down the buns and the condiments. By the end of the tirade Mary is back outside.)* Kenny you are not going to believe this I am fucking losing it do you see me I am losing it! It was the pink jogging suit lady. At our door! Only she wasn't wearing a pink jogging suit she was wearing shorts and a blue T-shirt. And she came over to ask us politely — sort of — politely if we could keep our dog from shitting on her lawn.

KENNY. We don't have a dog.

SHARON. WE DON'T HAVE A DOG. Exactly. And so I said to her, politely, I said "we don't have a dog" and she said "yes you *do* have a dog and it is quite fond of taking craps on my lawn." "Quite fond." Like slicing a razor blade across my face "quite fond." And I said "Lady, do you want to come in my house? We've got NOTHING in our house, especially a DOG. Especially we do not have a DOG." And she said "Listen, Missy." FUCKING MISSY! "Listen, Missy. I've lived in this neighborhood for six years, and I jog every morning. This dog appeared out of nowhere and started crapping on my lawn. I'm not asking you to get rid of it I'm just asking you to clean up his crap." And I practically started crying — look at me I'm crying now — and I said "Ma'am, people have accused me of many things before but they have never accused me of having a dog, you need to investigate further you need to knock on other doors — "And she said — her voice changed and she said "Look if it craps on my lawn one more time I am calling the police" and I said "Are you kidding? The police are going to fucking LAUGH IN YOUR FACE if you call them about some dogshit." And she said "AHA! So you DO have a DOG!" And I said "No, no, no, no, no fucking NO there is no dog here lady!" And she just shook her head and kind of kicked our plant and said "Ha I thought it was fake." And turned around I mean FUCK. KENNY. FUCK. This is like FUCKED UP. *(Sharon sees Ben.)* What the fuck happened?

KENNY. He fell through the porch.

SHARON. Fuck.

MARY. It's his own fault.

BEN. Can someone get me a wet towel? These paper towels are going to stick.

SHARON. Oh um, yeah, um — *(Sharon starts turning in circles.)* Oh wait also the potato salad.

KENNY. We only have one towel and I really think it is too dirty to put on your cut.

SHARON. I mean what kind of neighborhood have we moved into!

BEN. I think we have, Mary, can you —

MARY. Maybe we should move to the woods.

KENNY. Oh shit the burgers just a second. *(Kenny goes to the burgers. Ben tries to pull a splinter out. Sharon looks at Mary.)*
BEN. Ow.
SHARON. Yes, that's it. I'm moving to the woods with my friend Mary. With chipmunks and baby deer for neighbors. Fuck this bullshit place. Where nobody likes you and you get fired from your job because you went back to your car to get your weight lifting belt.
BEN. You got fired from your job? Kenny?
KENNY. Baby can we not —
MARY. Ha! Now there's a game plan!
SHARON. It's a fucking crack of shit, crock of shit. And I thank the pink jogging suit lady for helping me see the light of day.
MARY. In the woods we could eat rabbits, and if hunting was hard we could eat grasshoppers.
SHARON. And we can put a spout into the tree to get the maple syrup out. Do you know how to do that, Mary?
MARY. Sure. And just like you said no men, baby, no men, just you and me in our tent with our fucking mess kits in the mesh bag and the one pot and the one pan —
SHARON. And the sunsets shit there will be sunsets!
MARY. And no phones.
KENNY. The burgers are OK. They're well done but they're fine.
BEN. You know I think I need to go to the emergency room.
KENNY. Really?
BEN. Yeah, I mean it's not stopping.
MARY. Paul Bunyan! We can meet Paul Bunyan!
BEN. I think YOU need to take me to the emergency room.
KENNY. OK.
BEN. I'll send Mary inside.
KENNY. She can stay here.
BEN. No no no no no no. She's drunk.
MARY. I'm not drunk! I'm planning a trip.
BEN. She needs to go home.
SHARON. Kenny help, Kenny help it's happening —
KENNY. It's not happening.
SHARON. Just like they said it would happen in our meetings —
KENNY. Sharon —
SHARON. They said our old life would feel like real life and our new life would feel like a dream. I'm dreaming right now.
BEN. *(Through clenched teeth.)* Shut up.

SHARON. *(Starting to hyperventilate.)* I am. I can feel it. I'm dreaming — *(Mary grabs Sharon in some awkward and intimate way. Ben and Kenny are trying to deal with Ben's cut leg.)*

MARY. No you're not. You're here, Sharon. I am here. And we are going camping. For real. This is not a dream. *(Blackout. Night sounds. The lights rise on Mary and Ben's back yard. Sharon is tiptoeing onto Mary's back porch wearing a T-shirt and underwear. Maybe a ratty robe? Suddenly, Mary opens the sliding door. She is dressed in pajamas. They look at each other for a moment.)*

MARY. Too excited to sleep?

SHARON. Yes!

MARY. Oh my god me too! I can't believe we're actually going! Do you know the campground is only twelve miles away from here? I've googled it so many times. In case of emergency. I sit there and look at the website and imagine.

SHARON. I got hot dogs and buns and coffee.

MARY. I got bug spray and bacon and toast.

SHARON. We can make bacon?

MARY. I'm bringing a frying pan! *(They kind of giggle like little girls.)*

SHARON. I think nature is really going to help. Mary, every day really is a new day. But Mary, I open my eyes every morning and all I want is a pipe to smoke. It's like there's a fire burning in the center of my head, Mary, and the pipe is the water that will put it out. And I say this at our meetings, and they are all very supportive but the fire only goes down a little bit. Every day, all day. And in the middle of this burning I am supposed to envision my life, Mary. I'm supposed to set goals and maybe take night classes that will expand my horizons. And I guess that works, Mary, I guess so. But to be honest I feel like the real opportunities are the ones that fall into your lap. Like winning the lottery or someone's rich uncle needing a personal assistant. That almost happened to me once, Mary. And everything would have been different.

MARY. Well, now you're here. Things are changing for you right now.

SHARON. Mary, two days ago I fell off the wagon. I called in sick and walked down to the gas station and bought a stash from the kid with the skateboard. And I got high right there, Mary, in the parking lot by the dumpster.

MARY. Okay. What did you do?

SHARON. I started walking, Mary, I walked around our neighborhood, and nobody fucking walks here so I stuck out like a sore thumb. Have you walked around our neighborhood, Mary? It soooooooo beautiful, especially when you let the street signs really sink in. This guy in a pick up truck pulled over and asked me if I needed help — by that time I had accidentally walked out of one of my shoes, and hadn't realized it. So I said yes, please and he drove me home and we were hanging out in his truck outside my house and he finally said "are you high" and I said "yes, I am" and he told me about all the ways he parties — He does ecstasy he eats mushrooms and every now and then but not too often he shoots heroin. But he's careful because he doesn't want to get hooked on it —

MARY. Right —

SHARON. Oh and sometimes he takes ludes and sometimes he does whipits just to remind himself of high school. All like three streets away from here, on Solar Power Lane. And I said "what do you do for a living?" And he said: "I'm an electrician. I do house calls". And I said "how do you afford all that stash" And he said "Would you like a house call?" And I said no, our electricity is fine."

MARY. Sharon, I don't think he was talking about electricity.

SHARON. I know. But sex on smack just isn't my thing. And I love Kenny, I really do, you know that Mary, right? You can tell.

MARY. Of course.

SHARON. And so I said "do you want to be an electrician forever?" And he said well, actually, what he really wanted to do was be a marine biologist and we were just getting into this amazing conversation about the many varieties of sharks — the guy was rubbing my feet — *(Sharon starts to tear up.)*

MARY. When Kenny came home. *(Sharon nods.)*

SHARON. He knew immediately what I had done. He was really nice to the guy, considering. I spent the rest of the day drinking Diet Coke and watching *Jerry Springer* and then like four hours screaming my face off and trying to escape. Somehow Kenny tied me to the wall, to the door handles?

MARY. What?

SHARON. No, no he had to. He had to.

MARY. This all happened —

SHARON. Two days ago. Between the last time I saw you and now.

MARY. Jesus.

SHARON. I know.

MARY. I think I was at work pretending to type a letter while surfing the internet looking for plastic outdoor tablecloths.

SHARON. This is a nice table. You don't need a tablecloth.

MARY. I know I just get bored with it every now and then. *(Sharon notices the light on. She looks at it.)*

MARY. He's working on his website. *(They both look for a second more.)* And Kenny's still letting you go?

SHARON. Kenny thinks you're good for me. *(Aw. Mary is a little touched by that.)* And what about your life? Do you feel like a construction worker building a house, or a twig floating in the stream? *(Mary laughs.)*

MARY. You say some funny things sometimes.

SHARON. Washing our faces in the fresh water. Gathering a few nuts.

MARY. Sharon.

SHARON. Yup.

MARY. Why don't you have any furniture in your house?

SHARON. Because we're broke. Crazy broke. I mean I'm thirty-one years old and I still eat ramen noodles for dinner a lot. Because we have to.

MARY. What's going to happen to you?

SHARON. What do you mean?

MARY. I just ... I don't understand ... how you and Kenny ... are ever ... I mean something's going to happen again ... and you're going to be ... I mean how many times do you get to ...

SHARON. You've got to live this moment, Mary. That's all you can do. I'm as beautiful on the inside as you are. *(Sharon touches Mary's face. The sliding glass door opens. Ben comes out. He is wearing a cast on one leg. He's not alarmed, just curious.)*

BEN. What's going on?

MARY. We're too excited to sleep!

BEN. You girls are going to get eaten by bears!

SHARON. Stop it! I hate bears.

MARY. There's no *bears* around here. Sheesh.

BEN. Come get some sleep.

MARY. Good night, Sharon. *(Sharon mumbles good night. Mary and Ben go inside. Sharon scratches each of her arms. She goes towards her back yard. Blackout. What are the sounds? Is it the neighborhood sounds only processed? Or is it construction sounds, because they are knocking down the house a few blocks over? The lights rise on Mary and Ben's front yard. Kenny and Ben are sitting on the front steps of Ben's house. Ben has a light cast or brace on leg almost up to his knee. It is the afternoon. They are each drinking a beer, like a Budweiser. They are quiet for a couple seconds.)*

KENNY. Well whatever new job I get they're gonna garnish the paychecks.

BEN. Have you ever thought of sitting down with a credit specialist?

KENNY. I thought I *was* sitting down with a credit specialist.

BEN. And how much do those specialists usually cost? When you pay full price? *(Silence for a moment.)* I'm not asking for a lot of money. I just need to place some value on my time. Services cost money. If you offer something for free, it is seen as having less value. My book told me this.

KENNY. How is twenty-five dollars going to make a difference to you right now?

BEN. It's the principle. I've got to stick by my principles. *(They both take a sip of beer.)* It's not a lot of money.

KENNY. Let's see, we'll see. I've got a court case I'm waiting on in Arkansas. It's gonna save us, if it comes through.

BEN. In Arkansas?

KENNY. I slipped and fell in a supermarket a few years ago. That's how I hurt my back. That's why I have to wear the weightlifting belt. The belt that cost me my job.

BEN. Right.

KENNY. When I get that settlement, I'll give you your twenty-five dollars and you can give me more "advice."

BEN. Alright. *(A few seconds.)* Are you supposed to be drinking that?

KENNY. One is OK. *(They sip.)* So are you ready to start taking "real" clients?

BEN. I better. I have one more month of severance pay.

KENNY. One more month and you'll be just like me.

BEN. I guess so, yeah.

KENNY. Bruh-thaaaz. *(Ben and Kenny clink beer cans.)* How much you want to bet they're gonna call us any minute. Ah! There's snakes! There's roaches!

BEN. I don't know that their cell phones work out there.

KENNY. "Come out here! It's dark!" And you know what, we're not gonna go.

BEN. Well —

KENNY. No really, they're out there in nature, sitting in the menstrual hut, eating crickets, whatever, that's what they want, and we have to honor that. We have to let the women be women.

BEN. They better not come back wanting to burn that … that …

KENNY. Sage stick.

BEN. Yeah! I went to a wedding once where they did that. So weird.

KENNY. That stuff stinks.

BEN. Wearing feathers and a deerskin skirt. *(They both laugh.)*

KENNY. So whaddaya say, brothah? Boys night out. There's Dan's Place and Déjà vu and Temptations and Barely Legal.

BEN. I don't know — really?

KENNY. I've only been to Dan's Place and Déjà vu. Déjà vu is upscale but Dan's Place is traaa-shee!

BEN. I mean really I should work.

KENNY. Work? It's Saturday. Our wives are away —

BEN. I know but maybe —

KENNY. We're just embracing our human nature, man —

BEN. But Kenny those clubs are expensive.

KENNY. We're just relaxing after a hard week's work.

BEN. The drinks alone are like nine bucks. And it's usually a three-drink minimum. It adds up, and then what?

KENNY. Aw man.

BEN. You gotta stay focused.

KENNY. Aw man is that what this is about? You think its irresponsible?

BEN. I didn't say that.

KENNY. For us to have a night out? For ME to have a night out?

BEN. Kenny, look at the big picture. If we take a step back for a second —

KENNY. Oh god that fucking book!

BEN. I have a vision for my life, Kenny.

KENNY. So do I, douchebag.

BEN. Hey, hey. This is … What just … This is coming out wrong. I mean I don't even … can we … can we just drink, please?

KENNY. Hmph. *(Both men take a sip.)* You're a good man, Ben.

BEN. I don't know.

KENNY. No really, you are.

BEN. In a parallel universe I'm a good man.

KENNY. I'm an asshole.

BEN. No you're not.

KENNY. I'm like "You too good for yellow mustard!?" right in the middle of the store.

BEN. You're under a lot of stress.

KENNY. I'm an *asshole,* and it's too late for me. *(Ben doesn't know what to say. The two men sip their beers.)*

BEN. I think this might be against the law.

KENNY. What?

BEN. Drinking beers in the front yard.

KENNY. You own this house right?

BEN. Of course. Well I mean the bank owns it —

KENNY. Shit then, private property. You gotta hang on to this house, Ben.

BEN. Of course.

KENNY. Don't let anyone take it from you.

BEN. No, no we're fine. I mean we haven't even dipped into our savings and I don't think we'll have to. We're not ... we're not anywhere near that yet.

KENNY. Hang on to that house. That's what my grandfather always used to say to my dad.

BEN. And did he hang on to it? *(Kenny doesn't say anything. It is obvious his dad did NOT hang on to the house. Silence. Sound of the suburbs. Kids in the distance on bikes. A plane overhead. The compressors for several central A/C units. Maybe hovering a little closer than usual, pressing in. Ben contemplates boys' night out.)*

BEN. I mean I've got this leg.

KENNY. I bet it could get you a sympathy lap dance.

BEN. I don't know.

KENNY. I'll drive.

BEN. It's just such a hassle to GO anywhere.

KENNY. We deserve it, Ben. *(A few moments of silence where they kind of sit and watch and sip. Then Ben finishes his beer and crushes his can.)*

BEN. Alright let's do it.

KENNY. Serious!

BEN. Yeah, you decide where we're going and you have to drive. Except I've been to Dan's too and it really is too skankified so not there.

KENNY. You've been?

BEN. Sure for an um bachelor party.

KENNY. Yeah right.

43

BEN. So maybe one rung up the ladder. *(Ben looks down the street.)*

KENNY. Temptations then, let's try Temptations.

BEN. Should we get dinner first?

KENNY. Nah man let's just eat something here.

BEN. We've got nothing in the house.

KENNY. Fuck it let's scrounge. I've got a can of Manwich.

BEN. I think we have hot dogs.

KENNY. Yeah we'll chop em up, mix 'em around.

BEN. Spaghetti? Over spaghetti?

KENNY. Oh man no I think maybe no —

BEN. Alright we might have some white bread.

KENNY. My brothah we're good to go! Chow down and get there in time for happy hour.

BEN. I think it's two for one navel shots. *(Kenny kind of dances and sings that line from the song "Hey Ya" by OutKast.)*

KENNY. Awright, awright, awright —

BEN. That's what they advertise, anyway. *(This next speech cracks Ben up.)*

KENNY. See! For two brothahs on a budget! For two MEN whose wives are out playing survivor. For two men in need of a little R and R after a tough couple of weeks. For two men in search of a little good clean fun. For two men in need of a boys' night out. For two men who appreciate God's gift to this green earth: that special titty talent of the special titty dancer. For two men who want to feel more connected to their bodies and to the world. Who want to get out of the house and see the world —

BEN. Yeah!

KENNY. For two men who aren't afraid to have a good time even though their financial lives are swirling around in some kind of homemade toilet bowl —

BEN. Come on —

KENNY. For two men who are men. For two men who are going to have a great fucking night. For two men who are going to have a fucking great fucking night on the town, not far from their house.

BEN. It's all ten minutes away!

KENNY. For two men who can take one night to not worry so much —

BEN. Yes!

KENNY. Not to question so much —

BEN. Yes!

KENNY. Not to obsess so much about their lives and how they wound up here on Shiney Sun Lane or whateverthefuckitscalled, for two men who will forget all of that and go out. GO OUT. Go out on the town and engage with the night life, with the life of the night, who want to see what kind of *(Ben and Kenny almost say this together.)*

BEN and KENNY. Good clean fun

KENNY. Is out there!

BEN. Out there!

KENNY. And if in the process they get their hands a little dirty well hey, it was in the name of good clean fun. For two men who oh shit ... oh shit ... oh shit ... oh shit ... *(Kenny sees something down the street. Ben looks.)*

BEN. Oh shit.

KENNY. Oh shit. *(Ben takes the beer cans and tosses them behind the bushes.)*

MARY and SHARON. *(From offstage:)* Hiiii!

SHARON. *(From offstage:)* We didn't make it!

KENNY. Oh shit.   BEN. Shit.

(Sharon and Mary walk up. They carry pretty big backpacks, like camping backpacks, on their backs.)

MARY. We didn't make it!

BEN. I guess not. *(Ben hops up, hopping on one foot, and helps Mary take her backpack off.)*

MARY. First we drove out onto the loop and got totally lost.

SHARON. We thought we were going TOWARDS the campground but actually we were going away.

MARY. And then all of a sudden we were in this tiny town called "Sooter."

BEN. Oh that's where the minor-league baseball field is.

SHARON. And there was this store with a little lunch counter.

MARY. Can you believe it? It was like straight out of an old history book.

SHARON. And so we had sandwiches and Diet Cokes.

MARY. And the guy gave us directions BACK to the campground. And I went to pee and we got back on the road.

SHARON. And we were on our way and then I had to pee.

MARY. So we got off the interstate and stopped at a gas station.

SHARON. And I peed in this nas-tee bathroom while Mary flirted with the counter guy —

MARY. I did not! I bought a pack of Big Red.

SHARON. "Big Red"

MARY. Shut up!

SHARON. And then we were pulling out of the gas station and the car started making this crazy ass noise.

MARY. Like the gears were crunching together.

SHARON. Like the car was eating celery mixed with ice cubes.

MARY. So we stopped the car and the guy from the gas station came to look at it and he fooled around for like 30 minutes and did something with the gears —

SHARON. He rigged it with a coat hanger!

MARY. And we asked if he thought it was OK for us to take the car to the campground. And he said sure it should the campground is close. So we got in the car and we set off but we were really quiet.

SHARON. For like 10 minutes we didn't talk. And finally Mary said: Sharon, are you afraid of breaking down in the woods?

MARY. *(Pointing to Sharon.)* And she said: YES! I'm terrified! I never thought about breaking down before we left!

SHARON. There are bears in the woods!

BEN. There aren't really bears.

MARY. And I started thinking about my foot. And how I didn't have a clean bandage. And the wet ground.

SHARON. Slugs. Dead Frogs.

MARY. And I said well it's late so maybe we should just —

MARY and SHARON. Go home —

MARY. And right that second I saw the exit for Richfield Road, the back way home and so I cut across three lanes of traffic.

SHARON. I spilled my Diet Coke all over the window!

MARY. And I started laughing so hard I almost peed myself, even though I had just peed!

SHARON. And we kind of swerved to the side of the road. And BAM!

MARY. A flat tire! So I pulled over — I mean I've changed a flat tire before —

BEN. And you didn't have a spare.

MARY. I didn't have a spare!

BEN. I haven't had a chance to get a new one since we popped the old one.

MARY. And we cancelled triple A to save money so we were like well do we call the guys or maybe a gas station and WAIT for them to come here? Or do we HIKE the 20 minutes home?

SHARON. A hike. That's like camping.

MARY. Sure it is!

SHARON. So that's what we did!

MARY. We fucking hiked!!

BEN. *(Quick, re: her cursing.)* Mary —

SHARON. And here we are! I hate camping anyway. All those BUGS!

MARY. And rapists!

SHARON. Baby did you miss me?

MARY. We got cat-called.

SHARON. We thought maybe we could party here.

MARY. We thought maybe we'd grill.

BEN. We've got to get the car I guess.

KENNY. I've got a spare you can use.

BEN. Thanks, Kenny.

KENNY. Just a $15 charge. For the rental. *(Quick moment of quiet.)* Just kidding!

BEN. Alright let's go.

MARY. We'll get together some snacks.

SHARON. It's so weird how nothing ever happens.

KENNY. I'll get my keys. *(Kenny leaves and goes into his house.)*

BEN. We were going to watch soccer.

SHARON. You keep thinking things are going to happen but nothing ever does.

MARY. You don't watch soccer.

BEN. Kenny likes soccer. He lived in Ireland for a year when he was a kid.

SHARON. No he didn't.

BEN. What?

SHARON. Jesus that stupid story.

MARY. It's funny, just making the *effort* to go camping made me feel a lot better. *(Kenny comes back with his keys.)*

BEN. Alright well should we grill?

SHARON. Almost only counts in horseshoes and hand grenades.

MARY. *(A little over the top, a little dorky.)* It's Saturday night! Let's have a gooooooooood time. *(Quick moment where Ben, Sharon and Kenny are like "Huh? That was sort of dorky." Mary doesn't notice. Blackout. Night sounds. Then, the sound of music, low. Some kind of party music. Maybe music from Sharon and Kenny's Hotlanta days? It gets louder and louder. Lights up on Mary and Ben's back yard. Ben, Kenny and Mary are dancing their asses off on Ben and Mary's porch. Ben is dancing on a chair with his broken leg. Kenny is maybe fake humping the grill. Mary is spinning in circles. They are all beer wasted. Which is different from bourbon wasted. Bourbon makes you mean and switches on your regret.)*

BEN. Yay-eah, Yay-eah, Yay-eahYay-eahYay-eah.

MARY. I'm a sexy mothafuckah on yo roof.
I'm a sexy mothafuckah on yo back porch.
I'm a sexy mothafuckah in yo kitchen.
I'm a sexy mothafuckah on yo lawn.

KENNY. *(Wailing, high-pitched
R & B style.)* I'm your lover
I'm your daddy I'm your
car tire I'm your devil
I'm your sexy
I'm your burger I'm your
boyfriend I'm your superstar!

BEN. Yay-eah, Yay-eah
Yay-eahYay-eahYay-eah

BEN. *(Wailing too.)* I'm your superstar! I'm your superstar!

MARY. Hey Ben do this! Do this! Ben do this! *(Mary does some kind of dance move she wants Ben to do. Ben does it. Kenny comes up behind Mary and dirty dances with her a little.)* Wait everybody do this! Do it! *(She does a dance move. They don't do it.)* DO IT! *(The two guys do it, they are all in a line.)* We're on that show! You know that show with the dancers.

BEN. Yay-eah, Yay-eah, Yay-eahYay-eahYay-eah.

KENNY. I was on that show when I was sixteen!

MARY. Really!

KENNY. No. Sometimes I just say shit.

BEN. Look I'm doing the one-legged twist. *(Kenny cracks up. Mary twists with Ben. Kenny cracks up more.)*

KENNY. That is some funny shit. *(Kenny starts doing some weird vaguely John Travolta-esque humping of the air, almost like he is swinging his dick around. Or maybe using barbecue tongs as his dick?)*

MARY. Kenny!

BEN. *(Kind of cracking up but kind of like "what?")* Holy shit! *(Kenny wails and grinds.)*

KENNY. I'm a superstar!

MARY and BEN. I'm a superstar. *(Sharon enters with two bowls — one filled with water and one filled with some other kind of food. She puts them on the floor and looks at them.)*

KENNY. What are you doing?

SHARON. I'm feeding my dog. I have a dog remember? I'm feeding it.

KENNY. Oh that is fucking funny. *(Kenny gets two beers out of the cooler.)*

MARY. Oh right, your dog! You love your dog!

BEN. Ha ha that is fucking funny.

SHARON. Now I'm walking my dog. *(Sharon fake walks her dog, it is on a leash and she kind of dances while she does it. The others crack up.)*

KENNY. Walk that dog. *(Sharon walks the dog sexier. The others take up fake leashes and walk their dogs, dancing while they do so.)*

MARY. Oh no my dog just pooped! Look at me! *(She pretends to pick up the dog shit with a fake bag and throws the bag away. They all hoot and holler and cheer while she does so. Sharon steps up on to the table and walks her dog up there. Kenny hands her a beer and she gulps it down.)* Are you allowed to have that? *(Sharon keeps dancing.)*

SHARON. Yeah sure it's just beer.

KENNY. Her problem was really freebasing heroin anyway.

SHARON. Kenny!

MARY. That was a joke right?

BEN. Yay-eah, Yay-eah, Yay-eah Yay-eah Yay-eah.

SHARON. Yay-eah, Yay-eah, Yay-eah Yay-eah Yay-eah. *(Kenny gets up on the table and starts dancing with Sharon. Ben and Mary walk their dogs.)*

MARY. Oh my god I just got the greatest idea?

SHARON. What?

MARY. We should all fake walk our dogs over to the lady in the pink jogging suits house! We should fake walk our dogs over there and have them take a fake crap on their lawn! And we'll be like whoooooo hoooooo!

BEN. Let's do it!

SHARON. Oh my god that's hilarious. *(Mary, Ben and Sharon start to go. Kenny starts herding them back: he is a seasoned partier and he knows that crazy shit could bring cops and spoil everything.)*

KENNY. No no no we're going to stay back here.

MARY. Come on!

KENNY. Come on let's keep the party here. No no, come on.

MARY. Party pooper! *(Sharon cracks up.)*

SHARON. Get it? Party pooper! *(Mary cracks up. Mary and Sharon fake poop or fake fart on Kenny.)*

KENNY. Alright bitches! *(Kenny picks both ladies up and spins them around. The ladies squeal. He puts them down and the three of them dirty dance for a few seconds. Ben sits on the patio table with his feet on a chair.)*

SHARON. Come on Ben!

BEN. Just a second I'm resting.

MARY. No! No resting! No resting! No resting resting resting resting! *(It becomes a chant. Ben kind of dances in his seat. Mary couple dances with Sharon.)* Oh my god I really needed this! Some down time!

BEN. It feels good just to release! *(The patio table breaks and Ben falls to the ground. A moment, they look, just music, then Ben jumps up.)* I'm OK! *(They all chant and dance. Maybe do a little "He's OK!" chant. Ben dances with everyone. Sharon acts like she is holding a giant cup.)*

SHARON. Guess what this is? *(Everybody says "What!")* It's a giant cup of party juice and I'm drinking it down! *(Everyone hoots and hollers as Sharon drinks. Mary pretends to be holding something over her head.)*

MARY. Guess what this is? *(Everybody says "What!")* It's a big bowl of get down and I'm pouring it all over you! *(They all hoot, holler and get down as Mary pours the fake juice. Kenny pretends to be holding something over his arm, like a purse.)*

KENNY. Guess what this is? *(Everybody says "What!")* It's my hand basket and we're all going to hell in it! *(Everybody hoots and hollers "Going to hell! Going to hell!" Sharon starts dirty dancing with Ben. Pretty quickly they start to make out. Pretty quickly it is pretty hot. Mary and Kenny are still dancing and saying "Going to Hell!" Then, Mary sees Sharon and Ben and stops dead in her tracks. She reaches out for Kenny's arm, who is still dancing.)*

MARY. Kenny, what's happening. What is that?

KENNY. Oh it's nothing, nothing hold on. *(Kenny dances over and dances Sharon away from Ben. He dances with Sharon and whispers in her ear. Sharon kind of giggles and says "you're right, you're right" only to Kenny. Ben is shell shocked for a minute and then starts dancing again. Mary is shell shocked for a minute longer and starts dancing again. Kenny is dancing with Sharon, and when Mary isn't looking Sharon looks to Ben and mouths the words "Sorry, I'm sorry" to him. Ben smiles at her and kind of shrugs his shoulders and laughs back. Kenny and Sharon start making out. Ben and Mary get a little uncomfortable and sort of half dance. Kenny grabs Sharon's ass in this major way, like his finger is sliding down the back of her ass crack on top of her pants over and down between her legs. Sharon kind of rides his leg. Mary freaks a little.)*

MARY. Okay okay okay okay! I think we are stopping! I think it is time for us to be stopping! *(Sharon breaks away from Kenny.)*

SHARON. No, no, no no stopping! No stopping!

MARY. Weird things are happening!

SHARON. No, no, THINGS are happening. Can't you see?

BEN. It's OK Mary, don't worry.

MARY. I'm going to call the police.

KENNY. No you're not.

MARY. I mean somebody — somebody is going to call the police.

BEN. It's our house. We're on our lawn.

SHARON. This is nothing compared to what's going down on Solar Power Lane right now.

MARY. Yes but they do it quietly.

SHARON. *(Yelling.)* AND WE DO IT LOUD! Whoooo! *(Kenny turns the music up a bit.)*

KENNY. Just keep dancing Mary, it gets the endorphins going. We learned this in rehab. It can take the place of drugs. But you have to keep moving. *(Mary keeps moving: half-dancing, half-exercising.)*

SHARON. It's beautiful! You're beautiful, Mary. *(Sharon kisses Mary deeply. Mary lets her. The guys watch. Sharon lets go.)*

MARY. Did that really happen?

SHARON. Of course it did! Things can happen. You can just DO them. You have to just DO them. If you don't, then the world just stays the same. *(Music. Music. Mary busts a chair on the cement patio. Music. Music. Is Ben going to be mad?)*

BEN. Whoooooooo — hoooooo! *(Another mad round of dancing. On chairs, with each other. Nothing real sexual just mad dancing. At some point Ben breaks another chair.)* I hate these fucking chairs! Who wants a chair that you can break with one hand?

MARY. They were on clearance from Patio Depot.

BEN. Fuck Patio Depot! *(They cheer and dance. Sharon starts piling the wood from the chairs into a pile. Kenny downs another beer. Mary starts a chant.)*

MARY. I'm feeling, I'm feeling, I'm feeling, I'm feeling. *(Kenny joins her.)*

KENNY and MARY. I'm feeling I'm feeling I'm feeling I'm feeling.

KENNY. Take it Mary!

MARY. I'm feeling electricity, electricity running through my arms and legs —

KENNY. Yeah!

MARY. It's in my blood, the electricity is in my blood!

SHARON. That's good!

KENNY. I'm feeling, I'm feeling, I'm feeling —

MARY. Yes, Kenny?

KENNY. I'm feeling like my whole body is filled up with some kind of sweet air, strawberry air, and strawberry shortcake air —

MARY. Whooo!

KENNY. And it's making me feel like I can do fucking anything!

MARY. WaaaaaahhhhH!

KENNY. Look at me!

BEN. I'm feeling, I'm feeling — *(Kenny joins him —)*

KENNY and BEN. I'm feeling, I'm feeling, I'm feeling

BEN. I'm feeling like telling the truth!

KENNY. Yeah!

BEN. I'm feeling it!

MARY. *(With Kenny and Sharon joining in.)* Tell it, tell it, tell it, tell it.

BEN. Should I?

MARY. *(With Kenny and Sharon joining in.)* Tell it, baby, tell it. Tell it, baby, tell it.

BEN. *(Still in party chant mode.)* Alright! I have no website! I said there ain't no website! I have no website, I have no business cards I have no plan, I got nothing! Nothing nothing nothing!

KENNY. Yea-ah, Yeah-ah, Yeah-ah Yeah-ah Yeah-ah!

MARY. What? *(Kenny is dancing around.)*

BEN. After seven whole weeks. I've got nothing! Nothing to show! Nothing to show show show!

MARY. What did your computer crash or something?

BEN. No. I just. I think I don't want to, Mary.

MARY. You don't want to?

BEN. I mean I've got a domain name. A domain name that I own. On the internet. But I don't think I want to run a financial planning business.

MARY. You're telling me this now?

KENNY. *(With Sharon joining in.)* Ben's got nothing
Ben's got nothing

Ben's got nothing

Ben's got nothing

BEN. There's so much you don't know, Mary! Like Mary, did you know that I have always wanted to be British?

SHARON. I knew it!

BEN. Yes, Sharon, Yes! When I was ten I would watch *Masterpiece Theater* and read Agatha Christie, and when I would go to McDonalds I would order iced tea, because I thought that is what a British person would do. *(Kenny is kind of cracking up.)*

KENNY. Yeah!

BEN. And there was a whole year, when I was eight, when I ate all my sandwiches with the crusts off. Until one time I got beat up for doing that and so I stopped. Falling asleep wondering what a crumpet was.

SHARON. That's so sweet, Mary are you hearing this?

MARY. I'm hearing it.

BEN. And there is a website out there, Mary, called "Brit Land" and it is designed especially for non-Brits who want to be British. I have an identity on that website. A British identity. It all plays out in real time.

KENNY. Who are you baby, who are you?

SHARON. Tell us.

BEN. My name is Ian. I'm a prep school teacher. I teach geology. I like to bike. I have a cat. I am engaged to be married. I drink a pint of ale each afternoon. Right now I am asleep, because I like to get up early to go for my jog and a cuppa tea before heading to campus. Right now I am asleep in my flat.

MARY. Huh?

BEN. Right now I am asleep in my flat. With my girlfriend Julia. I spend way more time in Brit Land than I do on my website, Mary. Maybe more time than I spend with you.

MARY. NOOO! *(Mary kind of runs at Ben, to hit him. Sharon and Kenny catch her.)*

SHARON. No no no Mary. It's a beautiful thing, Mary! Mary, Ben just told you the truth. And now he is at zero. No website. No secrets. No nothing. And guess what, Mary?

MARY. What?

SHARON. When you are at zero, anything can happen. It's like total possibility.

BEN. Yeah, Mary.

SHARON. He's like a tennis player with his knees bent, poised to jump in any direction.

MARY. But what are we going to do? *(A moment. Then Sharon.)*

SHARON. We're going to start a fire.

BEN. Huh?

KENNY. Really?

SHARON. Yeah, just like we used to do in Plano.

KENNY. Yeah but that was Texas.

SHARON. Yes but it's such a beautiful thing.

KENNY. True dat.

SHARON. It's a ritual, a healing ritual for Mary and Ben. Their clearance patio furniture will go up into the air, like a flower petal on the wind. And then you will be at zero, together. Together, Mary!

MARY. Um. *(Sharon couple dances with Mary.)*

SHARON. We're going to do this. It's going to happen right here before your eyes. And it is going to open up a space.

MARY. What kind of space?

SHARON. You are living inside a tiny spectrum, Mary. *(She shows Mary with her fingers — like pinching her forefinger to her thumb.)* Like this small. And do you know how big the spectrum really is Mary? Do you know?

MARY. I don't know.

SHARON. Light it Kenny. *(Kenny lights a match. Somehow, the pile of wood instantly catches fire. A roaring fire. They are all mesmerized.)*

MARY. A campfire!

BEN. Woah. Isn't that kind of big?

MARY. You're taking me camping!

SHARON. Yes I am.

MARY. Ben, Sharon is taking me camping! *(Sharon hugs Mary.)*

SHARON. This fire is for everyone, Mary. For Mary and Sharon and Kenny and Ben. *(Kenny makes a torch out of a piece of patio furniture and dances around.)*

MARY. I can feel the heat. And the wind. Going into my eyes. I can feel my eyeballs and my inner ear, my inner ears. And I feel a splitting feeling, like maybe in my bones down here, the bones that make up my hips I feel a splitting feeling Ben? Ben? Where are you? *(Ben hugs Mary. Sharon moves away.)*

BEN. I'm right here with you Mary.

MARY. I think I am feeling another skin just below my real skin. It's been there the whole time.

BEN. That's beautiful. *(The fire is getting pretty big.)*

MARY. My forehead separating from my skull.

BEN. Look at that burn ... *(Kenny stands in the doorway to Mary and Ben's house with the torch. Sharon stands apart from him, watching him, transfixed. Kenny lights the curtains of Mary and Ben's house on fire. It's exhilarating. Sharon walks to Ben and Kenny walks to Mary to join them. It becomes a group hug in front of the bonfire.)*

SHARON. This is really happening, kids. Right now, right here.

BEN. He who hesitates is lost.

KENNY. Every day is the first day of the rest of your life.

MARY. That's terrifying.

KENNY. But it's true.

MARY. Yes but are the curtains supposed to be on fire too? Is that really happening? *(They look into the kitchen.)*

BEN. Oh shit look at that!

MARY. Somebody call the ... oh shit my phone is inside.

SHARON. No, this is good! This is amazing! *(Sharon and Kenny dance.)*

MARY. Ben let's go next door. Quick, let's go next door! *(Mary helps Ben off the porch. Sharon and Kenny keep dancing as the lights black out. We hear the sound of fire burning, of the fire getting bigger. We hear neighbors and sirens and the crackling of wood. We hear the shouting of firemen. We hear the "whoosh" of water coming out of the fire hoses. We hear the fire die down. We hear the neighbors start to disperse. We hear the police arrive and ask questions. We hear the wet wood smoldering. We hear the last cinder popping. We hear the fire trucks drive away. We hear the morning breaking. We hear no more voices. We hear morning sounds, pretty much like any other early morning in the Bright Houses subdivision. The lights come up on Mary and Ben standing in front of their burned down house. Sharon and Kenny's house stands next to theirs. Their front door is wide open. There is a man standing with them. He's dressed casually, like maybe a plaid shirt and blue pants. Perhaps the style of his clothes is just a little out of date. This is Kenny's great-Uncle. The keeper of the house Sharon and Kenny were living in. His name is Frank.)*

FRANK. I knew Roger best when he was nine years old. He'd come over to the house for Thanksgiving, and I took him fishing for perch a couple times — there used to be a pond you know, at the end of Feather Way, where they keep the bulldozers now. Got his line all tangled up in a tree. Fish hanging there like it was a Christmas ornament. Roger was my niece Donna's son. Donna never quite settled down — She had Roger with her first husband, and then she has two girls with the man I think she's still with now. At first his troubles were typical boy stuff — graffiti, cheap wine. Even when his son was born, when Roger was 17, it seemed like things might be OK. I remember he got a job working for a construction company. The young woman, the mother of his child, started cleaning houses. Sometimes those things work. Sometimes a child focuses you towards your life.

BEN. We didn't know he had a son.

FRANK. Well, he was my great nephew, and I wasn't that close with my niece Donna, his mother. She moved to Nebraska five, ten years ago. I hear now she's a high school guidance counselor. But I know Roger's troubles got worse. Drugs. And I think a spell in jail. Spells in jail. And so when Roger appeared on my doorstep -- all dressed up with that new girl — and asked me if they could stay in the house ... well, I told him I'd think about it, and give him a call. And I never gave him a call. It was a can of worms I thought best to keep closed. They got in through a back window I guess. I bet he fixed it right away. Roger always was a handy guy. Got in through the back window and then probably never locked the door.

MARY. He went by Kenny. He told us his name was Kenny.

FRANK. Kenny huh? No, it's Roger. It's always been Roger. *(Frank, Ben and Mary look at the burnt down house. The sounds of Bright Houses: cars, the hum of air compressors, kids in the distance, etc.)* Do you two have some help?

BEN. What?

FRANK. Help. Family, friends? To help you through all this?

BEN. Oh yeah, we have insurance. For this sort of thing.

FRANK. Insurance isn't going to bring you a home cooked casserole.

MARY. We're in a motel.

BEN. Our parents might come. And I have a brother.

FRANK. Whoo. Talk about a clean slate.

I lived around the corner for 29 years. We bought one of the model homes, the houses people would come pick from. There were five of them, and every house in this neighborhood is one of the five. Hard to tell now, because people have redone things, repainted, knocked down, rebuilt. But yes there were five model homes and you just picked the one you liked and they built it for you. You could choose your colors, or maybe move a closet from here to there, but mostly they just built from the model. It was no big deal that your house looked like a lot of the other houses. It was a new house! You were living in Bright Houses. It was like stealing second base. You were safe. They were magic times. Kids running ragged everywhere, skinning their knees, catching beetles. All the fathers pulling into the driveways at 5:30 sharp in their Belvederes, their Furies. Kids running up into their arms. Our arms. But now look at this place. Half the houses falling apart, the others so fancified they seem untouchable. *(He indicates a large house across the street.)* I mean how are you going to ask for a cup of sugar from someone who lives in THAT place? You'd have to buy a new pair of shoes just to walk up their driveway. This is not what the developers intended. They wanted you to have neighbors. They wanted you to be in it together ... Well I'm going to go down to Home Depot and buy some padlocks for the front and back doors. I don't think they'll come back, but if they do, I can't let them in. They've done enough already.

MARY. They really didn't have much of anything in the house.

FRANK. It's spooky in there. There's just a mattress and a coffee table and some dirty laundry. A few dishes. Sheet rock's all banged up in the bedroom. I think there's blood too.

BEN. They weren't bad people. They were trying.

FRANK. Mm Hmm.

MARY. We enjoyed them.

FRANK. Ma'am, they burnt your house down. *(Mary and Ben look at the burnt down house. Does Frank pick up an object from the wreckage? And then look out to the neighborhood?)* Someone should really start an archive about this place, and the things that happened here. I'm going to get my granddaughter take me on the internet, help me find people who lived here over the years. We'll track people down and ask them for old photos of the way things used to be. And they could mail them to me parcel post and I could glue them all into one big book. Maybe with memories written out next to each one. An archive. And we could put it in the neighborhood somewhere ... maybe where the old pavillion was ... and people could gather round ... *(He looks back to Mary and Ben.)* You know if you two need a place to stay for a little while, you're welcome to stay at the house. *(He points over to Sharon and Kenny's house.)* It's true it's a little rough around the edges, but I wouldn't charge you anything of course —

BEN. Thank you but —

FRANK. I'd like to help.

MARY. We're thinking of moving to Britain. *(Mary looks at Ben like, "right honey?")*

BEN. Right.

MARY. Ian's got some family over there. I'd like to have a farm.

FRANK. Oh well Britain's great. Beautiful place. Nice people.

MARY. Not really. I find them a bit snooty.

BEN. *(In a British accent.)* A bit snooty, yes.

FRANK. Oh well I don't really know anything about that. *(Mary and Ben look at each other. Frank looks at the neighborhood.)* You really should have been there. Two Saturdays a month in the summer time were the Noontime at Night Dances. They'd light up the pavilion with colored lights and you'd dance till you had blisters on your blisters. Everybody's shoes tossed off to the side. All outdoors! Nobody had any money. We all doubled up on babysitters — we'd pick up little Walter and Katie from the floor of Ed and Shirley's house at two A.M., three A.M. sometimes ... Such a perfect memory, sometimes I wonder if it was real at all. *(Frank seems to be leaving.)*

MARY. So long. *(Frank stop and points.)*

FRANK. I think I had a picture of my sister Lois standing right there planting that tree ... *(Mary watches Frank go. Ben looks at the list in his hand.)*

MARY. What's that?

BEN. They want a list of things that didn't burn. Something about our net worth. *(Ben and Mary look at their burned down house.)*

MARY. But it all burned.

BEN. Right. *(A moment.)* I'll do whatever you want. We can do whatever.

MARY. Well we have the car ... *(Ben and Mary look at the remains of their house.)* What do you think this was before all that?

BEN. Probably farmland.

MARY. And before that?

BEN. Who knows. The wild? *(Mary contemplates the wild that once was.)*

MARY. I dreamed last night that I was sleeping alone in the room at the Super 8, and someone started banging on the door. And when I opened it, and you were standing there, but it was like I had never seen you before in my whole life.

BEN. Really.

MARY. You smiled and said "Oh, I'm sorry, I thought you were my wife." And you walked down the little outside hallway.

BEN. I slept like a rock last night.

MARY. You were turning to go down the stairs when I woke up. And there you were. The real you. And you opened your eyes, and looked at me ... *(Blackout.)*

End of Play

PROPERTY LIST

Pan of steaks
Umbrella
Coffee table
Ice bucket with ice
Glass
Towel
Wire brush
Lacy tablecloth
Tray of chicken
Bouquet of flowers
Candle
Two-liter Dr Pepper
Huge tray of hors d'oeuvres
Pot of plastic flowers
Big plastic glass of vodka
Rusty cookie sheet, snacks
Cup of water, ice paper towel
Buns, ketchup, mustard, dill slices
Budweisers
Leg brace
2 camping backpacks
Car keys
Bowls of water and dog food
List

SOUND EFFECTS

Birds
Lawnmower in distance
Clanging
Siren
Sizzling meat
Night sounds: A/C hum, cars, doors, garage door, joggers, kids on
   bikes fade to crickets
Door slamming
Loud knocking
Wind, car passing
Teen laughter, music
Footsteps of joggers

ADDENDUM

Two Back Yards

To produce the play set in two back yards (instead of back/front), please make the following changes:

Additional prop: Place an obviously fake plant near Sharon and Kenny's back door.

Scene 2 (Mary, at night, banging on Sharon's door): Mary should not enter the scene from her house — it should seem as though she snuck out the front door of her house and has been roaming around the neighborhood.

CHANGE "I snuck out the back door and climbed over the fence" to "I snuck out the front door," so the line reads: "I snuck out the front door and just squatted there in the bushes."

Scene 4 (Sharon and Kenny have Mary and Ben over to grill): At the end of Sharon's dog rant, CHANGE "and she just shook her head and kind of kicked our plant and said 'ha I thought it was fake'" to "and she just shook her head and turned and jogged away."

Scene 6 (Ben and Kenny alone while the women are away): CUT the lines "I think this might be against the law" all the way through "shit then private property."

After Kenny says, "I'm an asshole and its too late for me," INSERT the following:

Kenny looks at Ben's house

KENNY. Look at that house.
BEN. What about it.
KENNY. You own that house!
BEN. Yeah, well I mean the bank owns it.

CONTINUE with Kenny's line: "You gotta hang on to that house, Ben." The rest of the scene follows as written.

'80s Pop Song

The moment in Scene 2 when Sharon sings to the group has been handled in different ways in different productions. Sharon might sing the line "Don't Stop / Believing / Hold on to that Fever" and then a few lines later Ben can respond "Streetlight / Fever." (In each case, the characters get the words of the song wrong.)

Another option might be for Sharon to sing "Oh Yeah! Live Goes On" and then have Ben respond "Long After the Thrill of Dah Duh Dah Dah" (as though Ben cannot remember the words).

It is possible that other lines from early '80s power ballads can work as well. Sharon is trying, enthusiastically and awkwardly, to encourage the group, and Ben is trying, enthusiastically and awkwardly, to join in. Permission to use lines from these or other copyrighted songs is the responsibility of the individual theater.

NEW PLAYS

★ **CLYBOURNE PARK by Bruce Norris.** WINNER OF THE 2011 PULITZER PRIZE AND 2012 TONY AWARD. Act One takes place in 1959 as community leaders try to stop the sale of a home to a black family. Act Two is set in the same house in the present day as the now predominantly African-American neighborhood battles to hold its ground. "Vital, sharp-witted and ferociously smart." *–NY Times.* "A theatrical treasure...Indisputably, uproariously funny." *–Entertainment Weekly.* [4M, 3W] ISBN: 978-0-8222-2697-0

★ **WATER BY THE SPOONFUL by Quiara Alegría Hudes.** WINNER OF THE 2012 PULITZER PRIZE. A Puerto Rican veteran is surrounded by the North Philadelphia demons he tried to escape in the service. "This is a very funny, warm, and yes uplifting play." *–Hartford Courant.* "The play is a combination poem, prayer and app on how to cope in an age of uncertainty, speed and chaos." *–Variety.* [4M, 3W] ISBN: 978-0-8222-2716-8

★ **RED by John Logan.** WINNER OF THE 2010 TONY AWARD. Mark Rothko has just landed the biggest commission in the history of modern art. But when his young assistant, Ken, gains the confidence to challenge him, Rothko faces the agonizing possibility that his crowning achievement could also become his undoing. "Intense and exciting." *–NY Times.* "Smart, eloquent entertainment." *–New Yorker.* [2M] ISBN: 978-0-8222-2483-9

★ **VENUS IN FUR by David Ives.** Thomas, a beleaguered playwright/director, is desperate to find an actress to play Vanda, the female lead in his adaptation of the classic sadomasochistic tale *Venus in Fur.* "Ninety minutes of good, kinky fun." *–NY Times.* "A fast-paced journey into one man's entrapment by a clever, vengeful female." *–Associated Press.* [1M, 1W] ISBN: 978-0-8222-2603-1

★ **OTHER DESERT CITIES by Jon Robin Baitz.** Brooke returns home to Palm Springs after a six-year absence and announces that she is about to publish a memoir dredging up a pivotal and tragic event in the family's history—a wound they don't want reopened. "Leaves you feeling both moved and gratifyingly sated." *–NY Times.* "A genuine pleasure." *–NY Post.* [2M, 3W] ISBN: 978-0-8222-2605-5

★ **TRIBES by Nina Raine.** Billy was born deaf into a hearing family and adapts brilliantly to his family's unconventional ways, but it's not until he meets Sylvia, a young woman on the brink of deafness, that he finally understands what it means to be understood. "A smart, lively play." *–NY Times.* "[A] bright and boldly provocative drama." *–Associated Press.* [3M, 2W] ISBN: 978-0-8222-2751-9

DRAMATISTS PLAY SERVICE, INC.
440 Park Avenue South, New York, NY 10016 212-683-8960 Fax 212-213-1539
postmaster@dramatists.com   www.dramatists.com